Thirteen Ways
of Looking
at
Tony Conran

Thirteen Ways
of Looking
at
Tony Conran

A celebration
in poetry and prose
in
the UK Year of Literature and Writing 1995
by
the Welsh Union of Writers and friends.

Edited and introduced by
Nigel Jenkins

1995

The Welsh Union of Writers

First Impression - December 1995

ISBN 0 9510337 3 5

This volume is published with the support of the Arts Council of Wales.

Design, typesetting and cover by Alan McPherson.
Published in December 1995 by the Welsh Union of Writers, 11 Wingate Drive, Llanishen, Cardiff CF4 5LR, Wales.
Printed and bound in Great Britain by Gwasg Gomer, Llandysul, Dyfed SA44 4BQ, Wales.

CONTENTS

Acknowledgements

The Welsh Union of Writers, and the editor of this volume in particular, are deeply indebted to many organisations and individuals without whose financial support, practical assistance and ideas this book, and the festival of its launching in Bangor on December 16, 1995, would not have been possible.

Warm thanks are due to our chief collaborators and sponsors: the UK Year of Literature and Writing 1995 and its director Seán Doran; the Arts Council of Wales, particularly Gwen Davies, its literature panel chairman Gwyn Thomas and its director Tony Bianchi; John Lewis and Gwasg Gomer; the Welsh Academy, especially Sally Roberts Jones (chair) and Kevin Thomas (director); John Clifford Jones of the Arts Council of Wales's northern office; Gilly Adams and the Made in Wales Stage Company; Dymphna Darcy and her troupe; and the Executive Committee of the Welsh Union of Writers, particularly Tôpher Mills for suggesting the title, John Harrison (secretary), Ifor Thomas (treasurer) and Robin Reeves who spent many hours transferring essays and poems onto disc with the 'scanning' equipment of the *New Welsh Review*, of which he is editor.

We thank the contributors to this volume not only for the alacrity with which they took up their commissions and met alarmingly tight deadlines, but also for their many useful suggestions. Grateful acknowledgement is due also to Les Murray and John Barnie, editor of *Planet*, for permission to reprint Les Murray's "A Tribute to Old Delight", which first appeared in *Planet* 66.

It was our intention from the outset that this book should come as a surprise to Tony. Our attempts to keep it a secret have involved all manner of subterfuge and shifty behaviours, including clandestine phonecalls to his wife Lesley's workplace, the burglary of his study, the (temporary) theft of irreplaceable photographs, and the quoting of his work without permission. We hope the intended surprise turns out for him a happy one, and that he forgives us our underhand antics. Lesley has proved an artful and entertaining partner in literary crime, and we thank her warmly for her ready cooperation in all aspects of this project.

Another key conspirator has been the artist Phredd (Alan) McPherson who, quite unprompted, offered to design the entire book, from cover to cover, and to prepare a printer-ready disc of the whole thing, absolutely free of charge. No one, for their generosity, expertise and commitment, is owed a greater debt of thanks.

Introduction

The UK Year of Literature 1995, beaming Wales to the world from its nucleus in Swansea, gives the Welsh Union of Writers an opportunity to do something it has wanted to do for a long time: celebrate the life and work of Tony Conran, one of the Union's most distinguished and active members, and a writer of Wales who is no less important to many of us than R.S. Thomas.

There are many, both in and out of the Union, who have long considered that Tony Conran's contribution to the literary culture of Wales has received neither the recognition nor the praise that is its due. With this *cyfrol deyrnged*, as such volumes are known in Welsh, and the Tony Conran festival in Bangor on

December 16 at which this book will presented to him, an oft expressed desire to raise his work into a broader, keener light moves at last from the realm of talk to that of action. We would rather celebrate writers when they are alive than when they are dead, and have established a tradition of staging events to honour the achievements of lustrous elders such as Harri Webb, Glyn Jones, Michael Foot and Gwyn A. Williams.

Tony Conran, translator, editor, critic, playwright, essayist, story teller, literary mentor, and writer of wonderful letters is first and foremost a poet, tasked from adolescence, if not earlier, to his bardic calling. When in 1954, aged 23, he entered a competition for an elegy on Dylan Thomas run by the magazine *Dock Leaves*, he did so fully aware that Dylan's death the previous year had created a literary vacuum - which he hoped to fill. Louis MacNeice, who judged the competition, declared Conran the winner, but the greater prize, the crown that Dylan had worn, was destined for the brow of a maturer talent, R.S. Thomas. As a poet Tony Conran had had little to say up to this point, although he had been a Welsh nationalist since 1953, and had sworn a Poundian oath never again to read Shakespeare for pleasure, the better to struggle from under the stifling cushion of Eng. Lit. The *Dock Leaves* competition was the turning point that claimed the poet in him for Wales. "If I was to be taken seriously in Wales, for my soul's sake I had to justify myself as a Welshman," he wrote in *Artists in Wales: 2* (1973). "Welsh culture had to be my culture, Welsh standards my standards: otherwise I was nothing but a charlatan."

He has devoted his life ever since to the investigation of Welsh civilisation, in all its variety, and to the creation of art works, invariably Modernist if not avant-garde, that rise to the challenge of specifically Welsh standards of excellence.

Tony Conran's journey has been a long and sometimes lonely one: he has been scorned by conservative retrenchers, begrudged

by schoolmasterly editors and anthologists, befogged and out-
volumed by lesser rattlers of the nationalist sword. Ever his own
most discerning critic, Tony once remarked to me that his work
was so Welsh that the Welsh themselves couldn't see it - an invisi-
bility occasioned, no doubt, as much by (anglo-)Welsh ignorance
of indigenous poetic forms and purposes, as by a post-
Movement and schools-led consumerist distaste, in Britain generally, for any poetry of ambition, poetry that is multifaceted,
uncommonly imaginative, electric with variegations of person
and tense. Out, therefore, with the likes of David Jones, Basil
Bunting, Hugh McDiarmid, Tony Conran - and in with the poetry of demure ego, whimsical anecdote, genteel suburban regret
and detail-obsessed imagism. (What a pity, it occurs to me, that
when Meic Stephens departed *Poetry Wales* in 1973, the bard of
Bangor didn't become its editor: with Captain Conran at the
helm we might have been sailing very different seas today.) It has
been for much of the time an unpromising literary climate for a
poet of Tony Conran's lyric and communitarian genius, but his
output has been prolific, his achievement unique and unassail-
able. He is one of only four English-language poets (the others
are Idris Davies, Harri Webb and R.S. Thomas) to have spoken,
on occasion, to, of and for the Welsh people, through means as
varied as his *Penguin Book of Welsh Verse* (1967), his "Elegy for
the Welsh Dead, in the Falkland Islands, 1982" and his revolutionary tragedy *Branwen* (1989), the most rootedly Welsh of any
play yet written in English (and many that have been written in
Welsh). Unlike at least one of this privileged quartet, Tony
Conran is able to speak of "my people" and include within his
generous ambit all manner of souls who break the bread of
Wales, whereas the exclusivist R.S., according to a speech he
addressed to the Union in 1987, is inclined to dismiss the non-
Welsh-speaking Welsh (and the Americans!) as English. It is typical of Tony Conran's hospitable imagination, as it is of his inclu-

sive aesthetic, that he is able to accommodate, if not identify with, all sorts of points of view, without compromising his own remarkably consistent vision.

At the age of 64, Tony Conran shows no sign of flagging. On the contrary, it's impossible to keep up with him. By this time next year the bibliography at the rear of this book, which we offer as no more than an interim report on an extraordinary career, will be perhaps half a dozen volumes out of date. Coming soon from this "Bendigeidfran of verse", to quote Menna Elfyn, are a book of Waldo Williams translations, a volume of poetry entitled *A Theatre of Flowers*, a splendidly irreverent *biographia literaria* entitled *Visions and Praying Mantids: the Angelological Notebooks*, the text of *Branwen*, a successor to his seminal critical work *The Cost of Strangeness* (1982) provisionally entitled *Studies in Anglo-Welsh Poetry*, a 'chamber drama' on the Nant Gwrtheyrn story of Rhys and Meinir, and what he calls a "Peer Gyntish" play about Taliesin - to say nothing of reviews, solo poems, reports and essays.

The main events of his life, some of which are rehearsed in greater detail in the essays that follow, may be set out here. He was born on April 7, 1931 at Kharghpur in Bengal, his father being employed as a locomotive engineer on the Indian railways. Wales, he insists, has always been an imperial country, up to its eyeballs in the British Empire, and in dire need of reneging on Britain and all it stands for. The wandering Conrans liked to keep a toe-hold in what had become their native north Wales, although Ireland was the clan's original home. Because of ill-health - he was born with cerebral palsy - Tony was brought back as an infant to live with loving grandparents, in Liverpool at first and then in Colwyn Bay. He was separated from his parents for much of his boyhood, and missed the sense, in his early years, of belonging to a community. In his comparative isolation, and from an early age, he wrote not only poetry but, ever the experimenter, all kinds of drama, from verse tragedies to bedroom farce.

From Colwyn Bay Grammar School he progressed to the University College of Wales, Bangor, where he took a First in English and Philosophy and wrote an M.A. thesis on "The Social Conscience of the Romantics". He became an Anglican as he entered college, but turned to Catholicism soon after he left.

It was then, in 1955, as he says in an interview published in *Modern Poetry in Translation* (Spring 1995), that "the catastrophe came, I ... found myself with a clerk's job in Chelmsford - darkest England if ever there was one." Though a dispiriting period, there were compensations. New working class friends helped broaden and deepen a political consciousness that has remained socialist. And in Chelmsford Public Library, with fumbling Welsh but a decent dictionary, he spent his evenings on the work that would issue a decade later in the *Penguin Book of Welsh Verse*; it sold 13,000 copies all over the world and made him famous.

His motives, as he explains in the Preface to the second edition, published as *Welsh Verse* by Poetry Wales Press in 1986, were in part political:

> My English-speaking countrymen in Wales were being treated as if they were immigrants in their own country, potential Englishmen and women who, if they persevered, might well inherit the green and pleasant meritocracy of England's nineteen-sixties Jerusalem .... If any separate existence was to be possible for Wales ... then the Welsh past had to be made available for English speakers. They had to be made aware that their own civilisation was as radically different from the English they were aping as (shall we say) Persian or Swahili .... Of course, I wanted a Welsh nation

created. It hasn't happened very much yet, but you never know.

His Essex exile ended in 1957 when John Danby, Chairman of the English Department at Bangor, found him a job as (officially) research fellow and tutor - in practice, "permanent bard of the place". In 1977 he and his wife Lesley were married; their eldest daughter Marged was born the same year, followed by Alys in 1981. He retired from the University in 1982, to concentrate full-time on his writing.

Formal Poems (1960), the first of his ten (so far) books of original poetry (not to mention his two dozen pamphlets), declares by title the centrality to his vision of poetic form and structure. Tony Conran has long argued, and his poetry has sought to demonstrate, that it is a sense of Welsh form and bardic purpose, rather than mere Welsh content, that will most fully distinguish Welsh poetry in English from the anglicising school of empiricism and self-expression. "The question we have to ask," he wrote in *Poetry Wales* 4.3 (1969), "is, not whether we can write poems about Wales - we can write poems about Kensington High Street if we want to - but whether our being Welsh makes us write different kinds of poems, with a different kind of modernity and excitement, than what other English-language poets would consider possible."

Against the routine shibboleths of subject matter, imagist verisimilitude, experience-fixated 'creative writing', secular common sense and 'unique voice' fetishism, Tony Conran argues for formal adventures, dream, intuition and imagination, the religious, the arbitrary, the social usefulness of art - in short, as he says in the forthcoming *Visions and Praying Mantids*, "all the things that modern English representational poetry as well as classical modernism tells you you ought not to do."

Although more intimately acquainted with, and influenced by

Welsh poetic forms than any other writer of English, Tony Conran is a thoroughgoing *inter*nationalist and shameless ransacker of other art forms, particularly music, dance and painting. Indian ragas, Kathakali dance, the music of Mozart, the hidden symphonic structures of Wordsworth, Japanese *haiku*, Chinese *shih*, the visual revolution of cubism, to name only a few of his delights, have been hardly less important to his synthesising artistry than *cynghanedd*, the *cywydd*, the *englyn milwr*. He has a profound sense of the interconnection and morality of art. it is characteristic that he should have chosen *All Hallows* as the title of his latest volume, with its connotations of healing, sanctifying and making whole.

It is characteristic too that as a translator he should have taken with such passion to the poetry of Waldo Williams, whose recognition that we have "*un gwraidd/Dan y canghennau*" (one root beneath our many branches) chimes with Conran's *hiraeth*, at the hillfort of Tre'r Ceiri, for "'The warm belonging root of us" (*Castles*, p. 19). As someone bereft of a sense of community in his youth, and as a poet-translator whose imagination has held him shivering in the darkness of Cynddylan's devastated hall, Tony Conran is moved by a powerful imperative to define and defend and invent upon this patch of Earth a place he can call our own. The building of such a Wales is not something, of course, that he or any poet can accomplish individually - nor would he expect to, seeing himself, like David Jones, as "adding to the deposit" upon which the desired nation may be realised. There's a long way to go, and not enough of the Welsh yet desire that nation; but their numbers are growing, and it is undoubtedly one of the poet's jobs to give the cauldron of rebirth a lusty stir. For Wales is a country, quite unlike W.H. Auden's, in which poetry has made a great deal happen.

Anglo-Welsh poetry has suffered a severe 'anglicisation' in recent years; it has grown stale and lost its way. If it is to have a future, if it is to claim the attention and engage the imaginations of the Welsh people, to say nothing of audiences beyond Wales, it is to the cultural analyses and empowering art of Tony Conran that the poets of tomorrow should turn for a sense of direction.

Over twenty years ago, Tony, you exhorted us (in your *Artists in Wales* essay) not to demolish, in imitation of the alienated loner of arty individualism, but to honour other people, strengthen the bonds between them - and give gifts. For nearly half a century you have made a speciality of giving gifts - poems to honour a marriage, a visit, a parting, a birth; indeed, your entire career has been a gift to our culture of inestimable value. In this Year of Literature, which has fair claim to the audacious bombast of its subtitle, "the biggest festival of literature the world has ever seen", it is time now for us, your fellow writers, to give you a gift, this book of essays and poems, to acknowledge with gratitude the fact that for the best part of four decades (to recycle your words for Victor Neep) 'you have centred us, your house is the hub of all Wales'.

Mumbles, Swansea   *Nigel Jenkins*
October 1995

Ambyr (i Tony)
Menna Elfyn

O bob maen, nid oes namyn ambyr
a dwria awch yr awen ddi-aer:
dynesaf ati, yr ystor coeth,
arbed ei chythru'n farus, yn ôl arfer aur,
diolch, am ei dal a'i dathlu'n lliw, a berthyn
yn ddieithr i gynfyd dan dalpfyd tlawd.

Adnabod hon, annarogan yw, yn sawru athrylith
sy'n amgau profiad. A'r pry, mor oesol fân
wrth ystwyrian gyda sglein i wehelyth nos
yr enaid, a'u gwefrau'n ffaglu ffydd
yn egni dirgel agored er aflonydd
cyn cloi yn gyffion cain dros arddwrn frau.

Glain yw hon heb olion bysedd
codiad haul yn crynhoi,
a'i gwasgfa'n orfoledd.

Amber (for Tony)

Out of rock, nothing but amber,
the trapped and airless gift delved out of need.
I come to it, that refined store,
relished like gold as it has always been
for its price, its colour that belongs strangely
to the cold stone of prehistory.

To know it, that shocking gasp of light,
is to catch the breath. And the fly, so small, perpetual,
frets burnished in that long night
of the soul. Amber that fires faith
in secret work, restlessly opening
before the bright chains lock round brittle bone.

Gem without fingerprint,
its glowing sunrise
is a pang of joy.

[translated by Gillian Clarke]

The Poet as Mentor
Sally Roberts Jones

In the summer of 1954, just before I became an undergraduate at U.C.N.W., Bangor, I found a copy of the 'Dylan Thomas Number' of *Dock Leaves* in our newsagents' shop in Llanrwst. There were ten names on the cover, among them Saunders Lewis, Peter Preece, Glyn Jones, Henry Treece, A.G. Prys-Jones, Roland Mathias - and the winner of the magazine's special Dylan Thomas Award, Anthony Conran. The winning poem paid due homage to Dylan's very personal style ('priest of the chapeldownunder air') but also spoke very much in its author's own voice. Louis MacNeice, the adjudicator, commented that the poem had shape, was "crisp in its language" and carried "a considerable punch".

At that point I had been writing for about five years, but the only poet I had met was the Welsh-language writer T. Glynne Davies. English-language poets, as far as I knew, all lived in England usually in London - so it was more than a little surprising to see that Anthony Conran had spent most of his life in north Wales, had just taken a First in English and Philosophy at Bangor, and was now writing an M.A. thesis on "The Social Conscience of the Romantics". The biographical note also explained that, student magazines apart, this was his first published poem, though he had had a poem broadcast on the Third Programme in 1952. (In those days it was not unusual to have one's poetry broadcast before it appeared in print.) Looking back, though I was much impressed by the prize-winning elegy, I am not at all sure that I expected to meet its author when I went up to Bangor. This was largely because of an ancient college tradition which laid down that male students from the university did not socialise with their female equivalents outside classes. This had more effect on the women than on the men, who were instead allowed to fraternise with the women students from the Normal College and St. Mary's at the twice-weekly 'hops' at 'Jimmys's' on Glanrafon Hill. There had always been exceptions to the tradition; old school friends, relatives and so on, and by the mid nineteen fifties the concept was fading anyway, but in the normal course of events it could have been a long time

> 1. Let images unfold.
> 2. Don't use too many compound words.
> 3. Revise.
> 4. Prune.
> 5. Don't gild everything
> 6. Avoid vagueness—test every phrase—but only when you've written it down.
> 7. Try to find adequate machinery.
> 8. If you can cultivate metre cold-bloodedly, do so.
> 9. Don't let yourself be led astray by metre.
> 10. Try to find your own personality in verse but don't be ashamed to find you are imitating other poets.
> 11. Avoid rhetoric except when it is dramatically necessary—poetry is vision.
>
> Tony Conran

before I met Tony Conran (if I ever did). Fortunately among my fellow residents in Bryn Afon Hostel were Margaret Bedell and Joan Hoy (sister of Peter); they had already been at Bangor for a year or so, and belonged to Tony's circle of friends. Once they knew that I wrote poetry, they introduced me to the group and to its leader.

In one sense meeting Tony was a daunting experience - I would imagine not unlike enlisting in the Marines. I had always written, but no-one had ever taken my 'hobby' seriously, let alone as something that could be a vocation, or that demanded any sort of commitment from its practitioners. Now here was someone who saw the poet's role in just those terms and automatically assumed that I would do the same. At his request (I assume - I can't imagine having been brash enough to offer them unasked), I showed him the two exercise books that held all my poems up to that point, and he wrote in one of them a list of guidelines for aspiring poets:

1. Let images unfold.
2. Don't use too many compound words.
3. Revise.
4. Prune.
5. Don't collect everything.
6. Avoid vagueness - test every phrase - but only when you've written it down.
7. Try to find adequate machinery.
8. If you can cultivate metre cold-bloodedly, do so.
9. Don't let yourself be led astray by metre.
10. Try to find your own personality in verse, but don't be ashamed to find you are imitating other poets.
11. Avoid rhetoric except when it is dramatically necessary - poetry is vision.

The guidelines were tailored to the particular poems under consideration, but they are excellent advice for any would-be poet; in due course I passed them on (with full and proper acknowledgement of their source) to my own creative writing students. Meanwhile Tony also published some of my work in *Omnibus*, the college literary magazine, of which he was then the English editor. This willingness to encourage a beginner was typical, and Tony took his duty as a mentor to the other, newer poets at Bangor quite as seriously as he took the poet's role itself. Although this mentorship undoubtedly owed a great deal to his interest in poets like Pound or Robert Graves, it also owed much to his interest in the Welsh literary tradition. How far his practical study of the Welsh language had got at this point, I do not know, but he was already using versions of Welsh poetic forms - in particular the *englyn* stanza - and in the 1954/5 edition of *Omnibus* he included a poem in which Gruffydd ab yr Ynad Coch "remembers his great lament for the last Llywelyn". This adoption of the persona of one of the masters of Welsh poetry was a stage on the way towards his own later translations; in *Formal Poems* (1960) he added the voices of Llywarch Hen, Huw Morus and Dafydd ap Gwilym to that of the Son of the Red Judge.

We were fortunate at this point because Gwyn Williams's *An Introduction to Welsh Poetry* had just been published (1953); it explored the Welsh language tradition in great detail, but it was also rich in parallel translations of the major poets. (And as well as beginning to make Welsh language poetry accessible, Gwyn Williams's translations were probably the first that could claim any sort of literary merit of their own.) There were two particular consequences arising from this: firstly, the idea of translation, of providing a key to the older tradition for those of its heirs whom history had deprived of their own access; and secondly, the idea of praise poetry and of the poet as a social being. Tony's

16

translations were to come later, but when I first met him, he had already taken up the idea of the praise poem - not as a celebration of patrons or heroes, but as gifts for friends or for special occasions - marriages, birthdays, funerals (which is where the elegy for Dylan Thomas really belongs, rather than as a 'competition poem'). And whatever Tony discovered in due course also became part of his protégés' experience, not in any formal way, but simply because he was - and is - a born channeller of knowledge and understanding (not always the same thing).

Welsh language writing was one thing; the English-language literature of Wales was something else. The existence of Anglo-Welsh writing as such was still a matter of vigorous controversy (and as far as I know, the English Department under Professor Danby ignored the subject), but in 1954 Bangor boasted an Anglo-Welsh Society. Its leading light was R. Gerallt Jones, and it had been founded to help ease tensions between students from Wales and English in-comers, a job that it did so well that it closed down c. 1955; I remember Raymond Garlick (then living at Blaenau Ffestiniog) was one of the last guest speakers. There was a small, unadvertised collection of Anglo-Welsh material in the college library, but the writers we admired and/or disscussed came from elsewhere. Dylan Thomas (not always accepted as Welsh then) was a giant shadow, and one from whom at that point we all had to escape; later it would be possible to look at his work more dispassionately and learn from it, but in the nineteen fifties it was the extravagance and the 'Dylanisms' that inevitably had the most influence on new writers.

Dylan apart, the main influences on Tony - and through him on the rest of us - were probably Ezra Pound (for his 'personae' and for his translations, but also for his critical views) and Robert Graves. There are certainly echoes of the latter's style in Tony's early poems ("To Erato", for intstance), but perhaps Graves's chief influence came through *The White Goddess*, with its exploration of early Celtic mythology, the figure of the muse goddess and the duty of the poet. (I remember Tony discussing this, and my own frivolous comment about having a 'red-headed muse'; I was more than a little taken aback to find my comment being taken literally and questioned further: could a muse be male ?) I found Graves's theories interesting but non-proven, but *The White Goddess* itself was yet another way into the world of the Celts and of Wales. (It is difficult now to remember how far Wales and its culture was a sealed book in those days; that Bangor generation - Gerallt Jones, Gwyn Thomas and, in particular, Tony himself - have done far more than their allotted share in opening the closed pages of both Welsh and English speakers.)

If all this sounds very earnest, that would be misleading. The students' union building was spartan, to say the least, and Bangor did not exactly have a café society, but the Bay Tree tearooms, down past the railway station, were a congenial meeting place. Sometimes we met in Tony's quarters in Church Hostel, and I seem to remember the occasional literary discussion on the fringes of the college hop in the Pritchard Jones Hall. (Wordsworth and Bill Haley !)

As time went on, the editorship of *Omnibus* changed, to Peter Arnott and Gerallt Jones, then to Brian John, and writers, too, came and went, some, like Tony himself and Peter Gruffydd (a.k.a. Peter M. Griffith then), to later fame, others, like Richard Hughes, Martin Likeman and Brian Wilkes to different, less literary careers. (*Omnibus*, of course, was bilingual; these were the English language editors and contributors.) In 1958 Tony won an Arts Council prize for the best unpublished collection of English verse; it was called, I think, *Sparks From the Stubble*, and was due to be published by the University of Wales Press, but although it got as far as the proof stage, the project eventually fell through. Another venture was a performance of the mediaeval morality play, *The Harrowing of Hell*, in Bangor Cathedral.

By now I had left Bangor and gone to London, for family reasons. About the same time Tony moved to Beaconsfield in Buckinghamshire, where his family lived; he worked, I believe, in a factory in Chelmsford. We did not meet, but kept in touch by letter, and he acted as a sounding board for my occasional depression, as a tutor, and as an unfailingly constructive critic. For this latter service he deserved a bravery award; I was trying various experiments, mostly unsuccessful, and his critical judgement saved me from numerous disasters. In October 1961 he also provided a list of recommended reading: Blake, Skelton, the French non-Romantics (Baudelaire etc.), Dante, Pound, Arthur Waley, Sir Idris Bell's translations from Datydd ap Gwilym, Rilke, 'the Irish poets', Edward Thomas, De La Mare, Hardy, Eliot, D.H. Lawerence, Graves, 'some Auden', Yeats, R.S. Thomas, Ted Hughes, Emily Dickinson. Interestingly, in view of his own later work, he commented: "you'll learn not to expect poetry of a high order from translations: that's why they are useful, because they stretch your own imagination: you have to create the poetry from scratch (almost) to see what all the fuss is about."

In the end I can only speak for myself in acknowledging Tony's influence on my work (which is why this account has such a strong personal element), but I know my own experience is in no way unique. This kind of influence is never easily documented; it is possible to see where one poet draws on another in their published work, but there are always other connections, sometimes even more important, but never written down. In this case I hope it has been possible to put at least one of those connections on record.

Marsh-marigolds: *Caltha palustris,*
Aberdaron (for Tony Conran)

Peter Gruffydd

Near a cold spring-stream beside a cliff-path
marsh-marigolds spread out over water
in juicy clumps, fat leaves branching
cups around closed yellow flowers.
They seem to shut well before dusk
scarves this path, seals its nightly
union with sea's reflective light.

And unfold after dawn when sun drops
a sudden arm over this silent headland,
lets warm fingers ease green sepals open.
Then this stream carries, in its preoccupied
chill pace to the shore, a crown, diadems
of such gold you and I swore to abjure,
oh, years ago, by the college by the sea.

Yet gold is what I think of now, marigold's
tense calyx, remembering those years,
your muses - so hard to keep track of -
and that one sure direction you clung to:
mastery, no less, a road that leads to humility.
Such advices as nature gives you drew
my eyes to: quiet fern, moss, unspeakable rock.

Above Aberdaron I watch for these flowers'
half-opening, become, on a deserted, early
path, some semi-fossilised spectator, witness,
discerning mysteries of matter's colour, form;
in its uncountable hours before an inch-slow
unfurling under a fecund vernal sun find
imagination's net full again, bellied out.
The catch is a rich treasury of years.

Our paths have led, still lead, in and out,
touch, cross at points, towards Cerridwen's
flurried skirts, Blodeuwedd, the Welsh Caitlin,
Mater Familias of our country's mazed paths.
This stream's loud reflection invades me,
my eyes are raced away to its lower fall
which nips eagerly over rock, drops with a choric
shout to a pounding bubble beneath.

If you should pause to watch that fall, immerse
your sight into its silver fans and ropes
then look aside, rock, fern and even stray
wall-flowers, tossed once as brittle heads
over the side to root and grow from stone,
lift, rise up before your astonished stare.
An old trick perhaps but one which catches
mind's voracious forays for meaning.

As these steadfast marigolds open I know,
moved on, your voice spoke to me
all those years of dispute and friendship
ago, that what it means is here in gold,
a deep butter-yellow which vessels light
in a trembling blur above that busy water.

Metamorphosis attends this country-stream,
while light over a flat and morning sea
is pewter now, an aggrandizement
of castles, battles, the eternal female,
and ends there in her endless forms.

Student of Translation
Dafydd Elis Thomas

Biography is not poetry, or criticism. Like all writing, especially the writing of history, it must be part fiction. Of all biography, intellectual biography is probably the most fictional. Memories of people, places, landscapes, rooms filled with bottles, these have a certain material reality, even as memory. But ideas? When and where they came from, and what the person who adopted them was like before he took them on to clothe his very nakedness - that is hardly memory. All this by way of apology from the middle-aged, perpetual, part-time student of literature to his old teacher. The teacher must be very old and venerable to have a book presented to him. To write in such a book is as we would write in a greeting card. It is a praise poem, not an elegy, but with a strong flavour of the particular affection written about between patron and poet - particularly so when the poet is a translator.

But a student of translation? Yes, continually so; it is increasingly a central obsession of a completely bilingual life. But I'm already jumping ahead of the theme. I am trying desperately to go in a straight line when my natural inclination is to go in two or more circles overlapping each other. The purpose of this text is to make it as a gift to Tony, my most influential teacher.

Nowhere is the excitement of the ambiguity of words, their conflicting meanings, their understandings and misunderstandings, more enlivening than at the point where two languages clash, collide and finally lie down together. But then an argument breaks out, as that play of identity and difference, which is always in and around language, starts up again. With the hindsight of (nearly) fifty years, I now know that this is the only place where I want to live. It is a borderland, which is also borderless, or where the border is rendered redundant, although bits of it still lie about in the field (an image from the Wales border with the Marches in deepest Powys where the sheep graze). To come to live happily in such border country is a life-long learning experience. To learn it in two languages is doubly necessary, though doubly difficult. For there are always people whose main wish is to disintegrate rather than integrate, to separate and divide, rather than discover a third country, where binary divisions are museum pieces.

By accident of birth, family, geography, demography, socio-linguistics, I grew up as what I now realise to be a natural bilingual. I can never remember a time when I could not speak English or Welsh. I am sure there are many such people, though few seem prepared to come out as the kind of linguistic version of bisexual. For those of us who have and enjoy that cultural condition, bilingualism - to use Colin Baker's fecund phrase - is a language.

It is no accident of geography, but a product of a very distinctive intellectual community, that it was in Bangor that ideas such as this blossomed. When I came across to Bangor (nobody could go up to Bangor) from the broad, flat bottom of the Conwy Valley, I was struggling to develop not only a personal identity, but also a social, linguistic and cultural one.

I followed courses in the English, Welsh, and Philosophy Departments, but mainly I followed student politics - it was after all the mid 'sixties. I failed Philosophy on account of the compulsory logic. I quarelled with the Welsh Department over the compulsory grammar. In the English Department I enjoyed myself as much as the staff appeared to. I discovered in Tony Conran a phenomenon that I never knew existed: someone who had been partly brought up in Colwyn Bay, and a user, no doubt, of that very public library where I had borrowed that early edition of James Joyce's *Ulysses* and read it every night under the bedclothes. In those intellectually intense, but always very funny, sociable and affectionate tutorials in that old hut, he not only took me back to the Metaphysicals, the Augustans, the Romantics, with his emphasis on genre and form, but he also took me on. He took on the very cultural and linguistic division which had bothered me so much in my grammar school days, and which still bothered me about the intellectual form and content of many of the other courses I followed. Gradually, he showed me bits of his work. And whether it was his own original crafted poem, or his own original translation, it was always the same way of presenting it. Not in the shed, but probably on the terrace of Glanrafon hill, or even in the Glanrafon pub, a clean typescript would appear, where the lines would be meticulously set out. They would be handed to me, and I would be given time to read. If I took too long or appeared too serious I would look up from the typescript at the sound of laughter: Tony, as always, being able to make light, make play, and fun, of what was an ultimately serious project. I could not believe it. Here was someone who had taken me through the classic English poetry curriculum, who was spending all the rest of his time actually translating, into recognisable metrical form, the whole canon of Welsh-language poetry which, I had been solemnly taught, was like *hiraeth*, untranslatable. Here was someone who was deliberately setting out to link up two linguistic and cultural traditions which I had been taught were to be seen as separate, and even separatist. Here was someone opening the door, lighting up a whole street, or indeed a neighbourhood, through his labours. And what of his collaborators? These people in the Department of Welsh could hardly be the fine upholders of an unbroken tradition, if they were spending time on translations.

25

It was the death of that greatest textual scholar of the Department, Sir Ifor Williams, which brought all this together. I was in my second year and editor of *Y Dyfodol*, the College newspaper. It was hinted to me quite strongly - probably by Gwyn Thomas, who was closest to me in age and attitude among the staff - that it would be a very good idea for me to produce a memorial edition. Names were suggested, among Celtic scholars, and Gwyn added *"ac mae gan Tony farwnad"*. When this elegy came I could not believe it. Here was the very imagery of the traditional elegies of the *hengerdd*, being used as a living elegy for their scholar. Here was a new English-language poem, which was also a strict-metre series of *englynion* which used traditional imagery, but which was also clearly a contemporary poem, with form and meaning intertwined: two cultures and languages intricately bound up in the artefact of poetry.

As Tony wrote in his *cywydd* for Bedwyr:

> So hard, to string in English
> The tied Welsh that I would wish
> And scan without cynghanedd,
> Heart's clamour, labour of lathe,
> Hammer-stroke - how I'm stricken -
> To give, I'm at it again,
> A mirror of its merit
> To the cywydd wild with wit.

So we would sit and discuss the essence of translation. Why was it such a struggle and a joy? When he showed me his version of Dafydd ap Gwilym's Morfudd *cywydd*, with its leading consonant of 'H' for every line, I could scarcely credit that he had done it with an 'S', and with the metrical and rhyming scheme also. "But," he would laugh, "Dafydd had full *cynghanedd* as well."

To see the typescripts of what was to become the *Penguin Book of Welsh Verse*, to be invited to comment, as if I had something to contribute, on the Introduction, all this was to give a precocious and erratic part-time student, even then, the joy of being treated as an equal. We never agreed on what translation was really about. There is no one way of translating, but a variety of trans-lating modes - phonetic or metrical or literal or prose - which may or may not correspond to the text being translated. I still think, though Tony does not agree, that his rhymed translations, with the replication of metre and rhyme, are the most difficult to attempt; but this is the only way of giving a sense of the style of the original poetic text.

Tony's highly original translations forced the English language to relate to the Welsh language in a new way. It is not coinciden-tal that the year of the publication of the *Penguin Book of Welsh Verse* was also the year of the last Welsh Language Act bar one. The phraseology of linguistic policy is not very elegant, though it treats of cultural equality. In the old legislation is was necessary always to refer back to the original, the original being in English. Now, as a result of the 1993 Act, in a case of a dispute between two versions both equally apply. There is no source language or target language, to use the jargon of translation. There are only two parallel texts in two equal languages lying side by side. Both are open to be interpreted and reinterpreted, to be read and re-read.

It took me years to work out the joy I felt in bilingualism. Language, culture and religion are bound up with each other, not in the sense that one language is a repository of religious truths, but in the sense that as the diversity of the Tower of Babel is itself redeemed at Pentecost, so too we learn that God speaks, if she or he speaks at all, in translation. Indeed all interpretation of language, or reading, is in some sense a translation. In every translation something is lost. But Tony taught me clearly, as his student, of all that is gained in translation. His translation, in life and work, was and is a celebration of diversity, an understanding of the essential plural nature of our cultural heritage in Wales and anywhere else in Europe and beyond. Louis Kelly wrote that "Western Europe owes its civilization to translators" (*True Interpreter* 1979). For Welsh poetry, in the English and Welsh languages equally, Tony has proved the immensely civilizing value of living in translation, from metaphors of decline and extinction, to images of growth and restoration, where the traditional form, and the post-modern, post-monolithic/monolingual, briefly and unexpectedly coincide. But perhaps it only happens in Bangor.

The Poet as Translator

R. Gerallt Jones

In the 22nd number of *Dock Leaves*, the pioneer precursor of the *Anglo-Welsh Review*, created and edited by Raymond Garlick, Tony Conran published a review of Gwyn Williams' volume of translations from the Welsh, *The Burning Tree.* The year was 1957, Tony Conran was in the early stages of his long association with the English Department in Bangor, and the review, although appreciative in general terms, was fiercely critical in its specific analysis of many of the translations. It was appreciative in general because the year was 1957 and, as Tony Conran says in the review, "I believe these translations are probably the best we have", and also because Gwyn Williams' previous volume, *An Introduction to Welsh Poetry*, had, again in Conran's own words, "given" one reader, at least, a delightful excitement, and encouraged him to explore a literature whose viewpoint is so different from the West European tradition to which he was accustomed". And in this volume too, "You read a poem, or a few lines, and you say 'How lovely!' None of the padding, the decrepit rhythms, the trying to force *cywydd*-couplets into Augustan octosyllabics, that one normally expects in translations of Welsh." And yet the tone of the review as a whole was, in the end, highly critical because the translations, in Conran's view, were simply not good enough, especially the translations of Dafydd ap Gwilym and his contemporaries, the high point of Welsh poetic art.

    In order to understand the significance of both responses, it is important to appreciate the inadequacy, often the sheer incompetence, of most of the translations of Welsh poetry into English verse which had pre-dated Gwyn Williams. Conran was undoubtedly correct that Gwyn Williams' translations marked a step forward. Examples from past translations of "padding, decrepit rhythms" and the like are legion, but it will suffice to note one or two.

This is how an anonymous translator, contributing to the third volume of *The Cambrian Register* in 1818 renders the harsh rhythms of Aneirin:

> And strait from Gilva's ambushed shade
> The patriot bands, with timely aid,
> O'er the bloody plain should chase
> The remnant of the alien race.

And this is how the same translator – presumably – renders Dafydd ap Gwilym in the same volume:

> Ah! could I tell the lovely maid
> Whose fair abode's in yonder shade,
> The converse I have held today
> With a staunch friar clad in grey!

(It may well be worth noting in passing that this is how Conran himself renders these lines in the *Penguin Book of Welsh Verse*:

> O that she who in a glade
> Keeps court, my famous maid,
> Had heard the fuss and blather
> Of the mouse-coloured brother ...)

Things had not improved much by the time the Rev. Edmund

O. Jones, Vicar of Llanidloes, published his *Welsh Lyrics of the Nineteenth Century* in 1896. Ieuan Glan Geirionydd's fine, if somewhat overheated strict metre lines on the Battle of Rhuddlan were similarly emasculated

> See, through the gathering gloom
> Dimly there seems to loom
> The sheen of targes:
> Hark, with a swift rebound,
> Loudly the weapons sound
> Upon them falling ...

The tight and often ironic sharpness of Welsh *cynghanedd* loomed dimly indeed in these translations: everything was reduced, by and large, to the merry trip of iambic feet dancing through the Celtic mists. Although things had improved a good deal by the time D. M. and E. M. Lloyd were putting together their *Book of Wales* in the early nineteen-fifties, it was still possible for D. M. Lloyd to translate those lines by Dafydd ap Gwilym like this:

> It's a pity the maiden who holds her court
> In the green bush hears no report
> Of my quarrel today on her account
> With the mouse-coloured friar,
> > which here I recount.

We are somewhat nearer to the intention of the original but no nearer, it would appear, to a realisation of the integral importance of rhythmic stringency to *cynghanedd*; strict metre poetry does mean strict. Nor are we really very much closer, as we shall see shortly, to the complex nature of the Welsh poetic tradition at the height of its powers.

In any case, it was in such a context that Tony Conran had reason to be grateful for Gwyn Williams' translations, and that readers of his own translations have reason to be grateful that he
came across them in the first place and by doing so came face to
face with a new and strange poetic tradition which was, he discovered, his own. For he soon came to realise, as he learnt more
about this tradition and laboured to read it for himself, that
Gwyn Williams' renderings were not adequate to the task which
he saw translation performing for the non-Welsh-speaker in
Wales. It is worth noting that the manifesto contained in this
review, written as early as 1957, represents a standpoint that he
amended very little as he went on to tackle the task of translation
himself, although he expressed it somewhat differently later:

> I cannot believe them (the translations) adequate to
> the task in hand: which is nothing less than a re-edu-
> cation of the Welsh people into the finer things of life.
> Wales has been made inert, not to say barbarous, by
> long neglect of her artists. The archetype of the *hwyl*,
> the revivalist excitement in a sermon, has made the
> Anglo-Welsh, in particular, an intellectually drug-pos-
> sessed riot of desolated souls. So long as a poem
> relieves for a moment the lonely ordinariness of our
> lives, we rest content. So long as it transports us with
> verbal opiates, we ask no more of poetry.
>   Now the real Welsh tradition, which these poems
> illustrate, is a very different matter. It is precise. When
> it evokes a situation it does so with all the gifts of
> irony, clear-thinking and intellectual delight. The poets
> were fine craftsmen; but their craft was not mere
> rhetoric .... It involved the clear delineation of the
> image, albeit in a fashion strange to the English mind.
> The technique was impressionist, in that they used no

modelling or perspective. The background and fore-
ground were joined in a pattern of wordplay, similar to
the brushstrokes of a Cezanne or a Van Gogh. Images
were used glancingly, not carefully placed or composed in fixed relation to one another. The brilliant
texture of their poems is not a fortuitous "extra"; it
depends for its effectiveness on a mosaic of themes
which together build up to a central unity.

This a perceptive and thorough analysis of the greatest Welsh
poetry of the fourteenth and fifteenth centuries, and what he is
saying is that it is the translator's task to represent all this faithfully, so that the non-Welsh-speaking Welshman can understand,
in precise terms, what the nature of his poetic inheritance is and
thereby succeed in relocating himself in relation to his own past.

Now, the Anglo-Welsh are in the Wasteland. The only
way to get them out is by showing them that poetry is
what it is .... it is essential that Welsh people be made
aware of their past achievements. It is no good getting
them emotionally excited over their glorious traditions; they are that already. The great need is for critical appraisal.

Why then should Welsh poets writing in English need to be
made so powerfully and precisely aware of the true nature of the
poetic past? The reason is uncompromising; they must know
what their inheritance is

if the Anglo-Welsh are to be more than a regional
curiosity in literature; if, that is, they are to make good
their pretensions to represent a national culture in a
foreign language. One or two poems, adequately

33

translated, and suitably publicised, could do more for Welsh culture than a whole battery of third programme entertainments on Welsh themes.

Translation then, for Tony Conran at this early stage in his career, was a mission. I believe it still is, and a mission that he has gone some way towards accomplishing in his own translations. The precision he sees in the Welsh tradition at its best and the precision he calls for from the translator is exactly what he finds lacking in Gwyn Williams' translations of Dafydd ap Gwilym. It is worth quoting his comments directly. He takes a section of Dafydd's *cywydd* to the Ladies of Llanbadarn and quotes it:

> Ni bu Sul yn Llanbadarn
> Na bewn ac eraill a'i barn,
> A'm hwyneb at y ferch goeth
> A'm gwegil at Dduw gwiwgoeth.
> A gwedy'r hir edrychwyf
> Dros fy mhlu ar draws fy mhlwyf ...

And then he gives Gwyn Williams' translation:

> Each Sunday at Llanbadarn
> I've stood, let others witness,
> With my face towards the fine girl
> And my back to the pure God,
> And after my long staring
> Over my plumed hat and over the people ...

And then proceeds to analyse it with clinical ruthlessness:

> Now this seems to me to miss the point at several places in the text. The ironic repetition of *goeth* which

34

can mean both pure and fine but I think is best translated here as chaste is obliterated in the interests of
adjectival variety. The poet is drawing attention to the
unfortunate chastity of the girls and contrasting it
with what he considers the fitting chastity of the
Eucharistic Host (God) upon the altar.

He has an even more damning, and absolutely accurate, point to
make about Dafydd apparently turning his back on the pure
God

> ..the translation of *gwegil* as "back" is positively
> destructive of the image the poet is seeking to build
> up. It signifies the nape of the neck: the poet is not
> turning his back on the altar, only his head. The trans-
> lator has either never been to Church, or never looked
> round in Church at a pretty face in the row behind: to
> stand askew a congregation is an action requiring
> moral fervour of a most extravagant kind; but to
> squint behind you is the simplest thing imaginable.
> Indeed Dafydd as good as tells us that he got a crick
> in the neck ...

I have spent some time over this early review, because I think it
brings two things clearly to light: Tony Conran's unremittingly
consistent stance towards poetry, towards Wales, towards what
constitutes a civilised society, over many years, and the fact that
translation has been an integral part of his career as a poet. If
one wished to be unkind one could perhaps say that it has
approached the status of an obsession.

He has certainly written a great deal about translation since that
early review, and is by no means reluctant to express his views
about other writers' efforts at translation; his views are often

trenchant, but always perceptive and always the fruit of his own deep commitment to translation and of long hours wrestling with it and meditating upon how best a particular task could be accomplished. A piece written for the *Anglo-Welsh Review* much later than his early dissection of Gwyn Williams and published in 1984, also gives an interesting insight into at least one aspect of his own approach to translation. We are once more in the presence of his beloved Dafydd, and he is reviewing Rachel Bromwich's translations of Dafydd's poems, published by Gomer; he is not pleased.

He deals first of all, however, with a certain Karen Thomas, who has brought up the old chestnut of the untranslatability of poetry in the course of a review of a book on the Cynfeirdd, quoting the famous line "Stauell Gyndylan ys tywyll heno" as an example, and citing tywyll in particular as an untranslatable word, its associations in Welsh being substantially different from the parallel associations of the word 'dark' in English. He allows the point to some extent, but in allowing it makes two positive and important points of his own in regard to translation:

> Ultimately you cannot make a Welsh (or a Swahili) poem in the English language. But it (the view that poetry is untranslatable), does ignore both the creative importance of translation, and the way some translation goes into our appreciation of any poem whatsoever. To give examples from English of the first point: the words "shepherd" and "peace", good English words as they are, resonate with vibrations derived from Hebrew ... and Italian ... in any culturally literate English ear ...

And he develops the second point at greater length and to considerable effect:

36

... some kind of translation is involved in any understanding of any utterance, and therefore in any appreciation of any poem. If "dark" carries all the luggage
that Karen Thomas says it does (she had referred to
its use in Milton, Blake, Shakespeare, Dickens et al)
what happens when we meet the word in Anglo-
Saxon or in Chaucer?... And does a twentieth century
Welshman reading *tywyll* in this ninth or tenth century poem have to ignore its connnotations in
Pantycelyn or Williams Parry wherever? ... English
can - because it too has its dark age roots - encompass this sort of thing, though for an English writer of
the twentieth century to do so is obviously a problem
of tact and creative impersonation ...

He then goes on to explain how he would employ this element of
creative impersonation in tackling the task of translating Dafydd
ap Gwilym:

... it would seem to me obvious that to translate
Dafydd - in so very histrionic a poet - one has to pretend to *be* Dafydd. I didn't actually go round the
countryside talking to salmon and seagulls, getting wet
under young ladies' eaves, chatting up girls in pubs,
being cursed by English travelling salesmen, ogling
women in church - or, second thoughts perhaps, I did
after all! But when I tried to translate his poems, yes, I
tried to act him doing those things, and at the same
time being the greatest poet, and the most original, of
his age, an aristocrat with very ambiguous feelings
towards English occupation, priests and his own poetic tradition. The two criteria are tact and creative

impersonation. And tact includes scholarship and verbal accuracy: that way-round, and not the other ...

As he has found in Gwyn Williams, he finds much amiss with
Rachel Bromwich's translations, but what riles him most about
them, it seems to me, is a notable lack of this creative impersonation. He quotes part of her translation of the *cywydd* to "The
Seagull":

> I love her, with passion's full support;
> ah, men, there never loved -
> nor Myrddin with his goodly flattering speech,
> nor (yet) Taliesin - one of fairer form ...

And he comments:

> What kind of seagull is going to listen to such stuff?
> "With passion's full support" indeed! Is passion a
> committee? Or a kind of erotic undergarment? In the
> dictionary, yes, "gwbl nwyf nawdd" can be made into
> "with passion's full support"; but it doesn't make
> sense, emotionally. "Nawdd" is of course the word
> used of the protection and patronage of a lord. In feu-
> dal times it was one of the richest concepts in social
> life ... And what about this "men" - "Och, gwyr"...?
> Has Dr Bromwich heard people - other than soldiers
> on a parade ground - addressed as "men"? "I say,
> chaps ... or what about "You fellows"? But "Ah,
> men", besides being too near "Amen" for comfort, is
> quite impossible in present-day English.

And so, while recognising Dr Bromwich's eminence as a scholar,
and accepting her superior command of Welsh, he cannot accept

her approach to translation, and condemns unequivocally "the critical naivety which still thinks that this kind of pedantic and timid translatorese is an adequate - indeed the only adequate - translation of poetry".

We have a clear idea by now of what Tony Conran sees as the central planks of the structure which the translator builds: scholarship and verbal precision informed by "creative impersonation". (His concern for scholarship is as thorough and punctilious as his concern for precision. His Appendix on Metres in the Poetry Wales Press 1986 edition of the *Penguin Book of Welsh Verse* reflects the thoroughness with which he had familiarised himself with the strict metres before adressing the task of translating them. This Appendix had previously appeared under the title "Translating Welsh Metres" in *Poetry Wales* in 1976.)

If we turn to the Preface to the same edition we will find a further development of the translator's manifesto contained in the early *Dock Leaves* review. In it he explains his motives for undertaking the task of compiling and translating the original *Penguin Book of Welsh Verse*, which appeared in 1967.

Firstly, he says, there is a political motivation, and he puts this rather differently in the Preface from the way he expressed it in 1957:

> My English-speaking countrymen in Wales were being treated as if they were immigrants in their own country, potential Englishmen and women, who, if they persevered, might well inherit the green and pleasant meritocracy of England's nineteen-sixties Jerusalem.

(By the way - if I may take a leaf out of Tony's own book for a moment and niggle a little - as a Welsh-speaking Welshman I always take exception to the term "English-speaking" to describe the Anglo-Welsh, as though those of us who operated on the other side of the language divide did not speak English. It would be more accurate to call the people he is referring to "non-Welsh-speakers". The rest of us are these days bilingual and although it may seem petty to insist on the fact, it is distinctly relevant to the anomalous situation in which we find ourselves. It is not, of course, germane to the present point at issue, although it may not be entirely irrelevant to Tony Conran's approach to the political and cultural ambivalence of some twentieth century Welsh poetry.) In any case, he goes on:

> If any separate existence was to be possible for Wales
> - as opposed to the shrinking Welsh-speaking minori-
> ty - then the Welsh past had to be made available for
> English speakers. They had to be made aware that
> their own civilisation was as radically different from
> the English they were aping as (shall we say) Persian
> or Swahili. Very little was available in English at that
> time. A popular paperback, a Penguin, was a chance
> not to be missed.

The second reason was closely associated with the first and had to do with the cultural isolation of Welsh writers who did not speak or understand Welsh and the importance of enabling them to express themselves as Welsh poets and writers:

> I have never seriously entertained the notion that
> Wales would return to being monoglot Welsh-speak-
> ing. In the foreseeable future my own tradition ... rep-
> resented the only hope of doing for English-speaking
> Wales what Joyce, Synge, Montague, Heaney and the
> rest have done for Ireland ... Culturally ... I hoped that
> my book would accomplish for us something of what
> the great translators from Irish - Douglas Hyde,

Augusta Gregory, Frank O Connor - did for the Irish renaissance. There is a great line of such men in Ireland ... (and so) ... Seamus Heaney does a version of the Sweeney story, Kinsella does the Táin. It is their patrimony. And therefore not simply a few names, or a story or two, but a whole habit of mind is available to Yeats or Joyce in a way that is almost inconceivable in English-speaking Wales.

The third motive is a more complex one and relates to what Tony Conran regards as a fundamentally different poetic stance within the Welsh tradition compared with the stance adopted by the English poetic tradition, at any rate in the modern period. This motive for translation he calls "the poetic rationale" of the book:

> The tradition of Taliesin, the great poetry of the Welsh middle ages, the defining art of Welsh civilisation, does not do what English education leads us to expect of poetry. That is my main reason for being interested in it. It is not simply a matter of *cynghanedd* or the twenty-four metres. The formal patterning of Welsh poetry reaches far deeper than the rules. The second person - you - is its main subject; but all three grammatical persons - I, you, her or she or it - are used as axes of growth such that different styles of discourse develop along each axis. Praise-poetry is what it is usually called, but ... I think I'd now want to call it 'boast-poetry'. It brags of its subject who is nearly always imagined as listening, and in fact probably did listen. It was, then, real - if highly crafted - speech. And as such it is itself a fulcrum for us. One can get a purchase from it. It gives one a criterion of

41

whole speaking, of making poetry as a private person,
a social being and an objective observer - all at once.
It allows one to judge the imagism of contemporary
English poetry for what it is - partial speaking merely,
framing bits of experience for sale as commodities.

All this obviously has immense implications for Conran's own
poetry, its stance and nature, but that is beyond the remit of this
essay, although it is difficult to resist some comment about direct
and obvious influences when one comes across a poem like his
"Praise-song for Eirlys" written as recently as 1989 and published in *Poetry Wales*:

> A court in Upper Bangor -
> Eirlys the lady of it.
> And before her, the good ways,
> The kitchen always open
> Of Anna and Mrs Daniel,
> Eleri Elliot and Non,
> Brenda, palette knife of words,
> Star Chamberlain of islands.

Quite apart from the metrics - a close approximation to the
cywydd's seven syllable line - this is the very stuff of the praise
tradition, reminiscent perhaps of Guto'r Glyn praising the Abbot
of Glyn Egwestl for the generosity of his hospitality to Guto in
old age or of Iolo Goch singing the praises of Owen Glyndwr's
Sycharth, and entirely apposite to its purpose. But such direct
influences on the poet's own work are for other contributors to
this volume to address.

What is perhaps within the remit of this essay is to note that,
time and again as we read what Tony Conran has to say about
translation, we are forced to recognise the all-pervasive influence

of the traditions and the very rationale of Welsh medieval poetry upon his own thinking and therefore upon his work. Interviewed by Ian Gregson in the Winter 1988 number of the *New Welsh Review* he appears both to reinforce this fact and also, in some ways, to distance himself from it. At the beginning of the interview, he returns to the question of a poetic rationale:

> ... I've been influenced by Welsh poetry to a great extent of course. But my poems arise out of a situation, out of a social situation. That has always been true. But to a large extent ... I've got to create my situation as I go along and if I am a traditional Welsh poet, I am by choice, by creating something where there was very little before. And of course I do so in an English context - which makes me a very strange creature as far as English writers are concerned ...

When pressed about this, he says:

> ... what excites me about Welsh poets is that they start with the community and the individual is always related to that community. Whereas the English poet has to start with the idea that he's alone in a strange world, he's lost his bearings towards the people, the most he can hope for is a circle of intimates.

It is not perhaps insignificant that another poet with whom Conran has a considerable affinity, and a poet who was also attracted to certain aspects of early Celtic poetry, Robert Graves, makes a very similar complaint in the Introduction to his *Collected Poems* where he compares the modern English poet to a brushless - and therefore rudderless - fox, a creature with no clear direction, role or function. When Ian Gregson brings up the question of Conran's own gift poems, clearly derived, however indirectly, from the praise tradition, Conran answers:

> ... if you're a tribal or a feudal poet, you can write praise-poems to a lord or a prince and that's really the end of the matter. That's what that kind of poet does. If his work is preserved, it is so almost by accident. Now I write in a specific situation. I write poems to specific people giving them specific things and perhaps that ought to be the end of the matter too but this 'thought that counts' can in fact be taken on board by other people who read the poem. They can in fact put themselves in that situation, in their imagination, and so the poem can be bought and sold like any other ...

This is a central concern of his, because he does not believe that a poem should be treated as a commodity nor should the poet be a trader in the capitalist market place. However, even operating within an unsatisfactory English context as he does, he nevertheless feels that, as he has lived his life as a poet in Wales, he has been able to some extent at least to reassume for himself the poet's social role:

> I do find more and more that I can act - however inadequately - as a spokeman for a people. I think my work - some of it - has been regarded in this way, as has that of R. S. Thomas as well. It's something the great Welsh language poets do all the time of course - they're felt to be spokesmen for the Welsh people. What they say has political importance, it defines a people's attitude to itself ...

And although he somewhat disingenuously tries to distance Conran the poet from Conran the translator towards the end of the interview - "having a reputation ... as a translator is in some ways a disadvantage because people think of you primarily as a translator and not as a poet" - nevertheless his final statement in the interview regarding himself as translator is a thoroughly positive one:

> It has its positive side. I know where 1 am in Wales now, I have the authority of the Welsh tradition ...

Although there are translations and adaptations scattered throughout his work (and not only from the Welsh: Nicholas Parry at the Tern Press, for example, published *Eighteen Poems of Dante Alighieri*, a beautifully worked selection of sonnets and canzone, in 1975) the Penguin book is clearly his major achievement in the field of translation. Bearing in mind the whole rich resource of scholarship, of political attitude, of poetic stance, of intellectual concern regarding the nature and role of translation that lies behind the work, a resource we have merely glimpsed in this essay, how does the Penguin book appear, in terms of selection and method, to one coming to it from the other side of the language divide?

Let it be said unequivocally, first of all, that it is, by any standards, a major achievement. In its 1986 revised version, *Welsh Verse*, published by Poetry Wales Press, it comprises an eighty page Introduction which is in itself a valuable and original overview of the whole spectrum of Welsh poetry, from earliest times to the twentieth century, one hundred and seventy translations representing a huge variety of styles and stances and some useful Appendices, the most substantial of which, "Appendix on Metres", had previously been published in the Winter 1976 number of *Poetry Wales* under the title "Translating Welsh

Metres". Quite apart from the quality of the translations and the genuine scholarship informing the Introduction and the Appendices, no one had previously attempted anything on this scale; it was and is unique.

It remains to comment on the selection that Tony Conran has chosen and on the nature and quality of individual translations. Selection, of course, is in the end a subjective process, however much one attempts to distance oneself, and reactions to selection are likely to be equally subjective, but there are some comments which should be made. By and large, *Welsh Verse* does display effectively the great panoramic development of poetry in what has been recognisably the same language for fourteen hundred years; equally, it makes it clear that poetry in Welsh is a living and continuing tradition, not merely a medieval activity that effectively came to an end with the accession of the Tudor dynasty. It represents the early poetry fully, and the inclusion of such poets as Meilyr (fl.1100-1137), Owain Cyfeiliog (d.1197), Elidir Sais (c. 1195-1246) and in particular Cynddelw Prydydd Mawr (fl.1155-1200), shows the continuity of the tradition during a period which is sometimes shown as a vacuum filled only by Hywel ab Owain Gwynedd. When we come to the great flowering of the poetic tradition from the fourteenth to the sixteenth centuries, he rightly includes seventeen poets together with some anonymous work. The only poets, however, who are represented by more than one poem, apart from Dafydd ap Gwilym (fl.1340-1370), whose pre-eminence rightly rates eight, are Sion Cent (fl.1400-1430), Dafydd Nanmor (fl.1450-1480) and Guto'r Glyn (fl.1450-1490), who rate two each. I feel that this gives an unbalanced view of this quite remarkable period, and a period which Tony Conran himself feels very close to in many ways, and does scant justice, for example, to major poets like Iolo Goch (c.1320-c.1398), Lewis Glyn Cothi(fl.1447-1486) and the poet who was in many ways the last of the great line, William

Llyn (d.1580). It would clearly not be Tony Conran's intention to present the period as one totally dominated by one major figure surrounded by comparatively insignificant satellites, but there is some danger of that, given the imbalance of the represenation. Moving forward to the eighteenth century, I wonder whether the prolific and many-faceted greatness of Williams Pantycelyn is properly represented by three hymns? I'm sure the editor is correct to skate over the comparative, if manically energetic, poetic aridity of the nineteenth century, and, in viewing the selection from the twentieth century, clearly the most fruitful and prolific since medieval times, one has to bear in mind that the book was originally published in 1967. Probably the time is ripe for yet another and more drastic revision than that which resulted in the publication of *Welsh Verse* in 1986, as a great deal has happened to Welsh poetry during the last quarter of a century, developments which are to some extent reflected in the recent work of the only other major translator from the Welsh, Joseph Clancy. Such a revision would enable justice to be done, for example, to Waldo Williams, Euros Bowen and Bobi Jones, not to speak of the inclusion of a whole new generation of substantial poets. The fact that one can particularise in this way, however, simply emphasises the scale of the conribution made by the Penguin book. There would have been no point in doing so before Tony Conran had first of all opened out the vista and enabled the non-Welsh-speaking reader to view the whole scene.

As to the quality of the translations, it is simply true to say that they demonstrate admirably the criteria that he himself has set out for the translator and which we have already noted. This is particularly true of the medieval verse, the praise-poetry which is so close to the translator's heart and its staple-product the *cywydd*. And of the poets of the great tradition, it is the greatest of them, Dafydd ap Gwilym, who has especially captured Tony Conran's imagination. It is worth noting that it was in fact

Dafydd who made the *cywydd* into the flexible all-purpose instrument that was to serve his contemporaries and successors so well. Up to his time it had simply been a somewhat crude accumulation of end-stopped rhyming couplets. By running the meaning through the line structure, much in the way of Shakespeare's handling of the sonnet, by subtle variations of rhythm, by developing the device of parenthetic comment, he transformed it into a highly sophisticated medium, suitable for his own complex blend of passion, irony and social comment, suitable for a poetry that was both deeply rooted in the tradition that he had inherited and much enriched by the cosmopolitan influences that had borne in upon Dafydd himself. Let us see how Tony Conran handles the *cywydd* which he had berated Gwyn Williams for doing less than justice to, "The Ladies of Llanbadarn". Here is the relevant section:

> In Llanbadarn every Sunday
> Was I, and (judge who may)
> Towards chaste girls I faced,
> My nape to a God rightly chaste,
> And through my plumes gazed long
> At that religious throng.

And he continues in the same vein, using a consistent two-stress line taking as its norm the seven-syllable *cywydd* couplet, but where necessary extending it to eight syllables or conracting it to six:

> One gay bright girl says on
> To t'other prudent-prospering one -
>
> That pale and flirt-faced lad
> With hair from his sister's head -

> Adulterous must be the gaze
> Of a fellow with such ways.
> 'Is he that sort?' demands
> The girl on her right hand,
> 'Be damned to him, he'll stay
> Unanswered till Judgement day!'

I believe that this catches as exactly as is possible in English, both the dominant rhythm of the original and at the same time its flexibility and its sense of natural speech. The same is true, for example, of his rendering of one of the great *cywyddau* of a hundred years later, Guto'r Glyn's tribute to Dafydd ab Ieuan, Abbot of Glyn Egwestl, "In His Old Age and Blindness":

> Where are the old men? Dead, at last?
> I tonight am left the oldest.
> I was given more than my share
> Of old age and bad temper -
> A talkative man, and often
> Rambling on about old men,
> Like the all-too-eloquent tongue,
> All summer, of Rhys Bwtlwng.
> What babbles is the burden
> Of my lack of these good men.
> It's tiresome, like prentice wit,
> That old fools won't be quiet,
> But more so, the blind man's plight
> If not dumb, kept from daylight.

It goes without saying that the translator is absolutely right not to try to represent the cadences of *cynghanedd* in English; *cynghanedd* in English simply sounds comic; it is far more important to get the spirit and the rhythmic movement right.

The translations are also strong in their presentation of the early heroic poetry. The stark simplicity of Llywarch Hen's complaint regarding the onset of old age seems to me to have been captured precisely:

> Ere my back was bent, I was brilliant.
> My spear was the first to strike.
> A hunchback now, I am heavy and wretched.
>
> Wooden crook, it is autumn.
> Bracken red, stubble sere,
> I've surrendered all I love.
>
> Wooden crook, it is winter.
> Men shout gaily over the drink,
> At my bedside, no one greets me.

When it comes to representing the fractured tradition of the twentieth century, and the often more ambivalent and individualistic poetry of our own time, I am not always so confident that he is equally at ease. There are certainly distinguished twentieth century translations in the book, notably and perhaps significantly the poems of Saunders Lewis, but the sense of immediate and joyous identification which one finds in the poems of the great tradition is not so recognisable here. What is clearly there all the time, however, is the conscious craft, the care, the precision, the attention to detail.

For Tony Conran, the craftsmanship is fundamental and it cannot be overstressed that the quality of translation which is almost always present in his work cannot be achieved without the concealed meticulous care that prepares the way for it. This is evident, both in a positive and in a negative sense in translations by him not included in the Penguin book and its successor, but published in the *New Welsh Review* for Winter 1990-91. On the one hand, there is a translation of a poem by Waldo Williams which is clearly the result of this exceptional attention to detail, and on the other hand a translation of another poem by the same poet where Homer for once, in my view, nods.

In the one case, "Tri Bardd o Sais a Lloegr" (Three English Poets and England), the translation, an excellent one in my view, throwing new light on certain aspects of the poem, is accompanied by an article tracing its biographical background and relating it convincingly to areas of Waldo's life which have remained to an extent in shadow. In the other case, "Eirlysiau" (Snowdrops), a short poem with which I have myself grappled at various times, either the translator falls short of his own exceptional standards or else I have quite mistaken his intentions.

The first stanza of this poem, in the original, reads as follows:

> Gwyn, gwyn,
> Yw'r gynnar dorf ar lawr y glyn,
> O'r ddaear ddu y nef a'i mynn,
> Golau a'u pryn o'u gwely pridd,
> A rhed y gwanwyn yn ddiglwy
> O'u cyffro hwy uwch cae a ffridd.

Tony Conran renders it like this:

> Very holy
> That first hosting down the valley.
> Out of black earth, sky calls them.
> It's light wins them from the mould.
> Springtime runs untainted in their white.
> They wake over high pasture and field.

There are a number of matters I would take issue with in this rendering; I will mention one or two. When I wrote a brief essay on this poem some years ago, drawing attention to the fact that its imagery built up a powerful picture of the dead rising from their graves on the Day of Judgement, Waldo, in his usual gently provocative manner, pointed out that it was, in the first instance simply a poem about snowdrops. Which of course it is! The dictionary translation of the first two lines is "White, white, the early crowd on the floor of the valley". The snowdrops, spread out along the valley floor, were startlingly white. I cannot see why the "early crowd" should need to be transformed into "That first hosting". But there are more serious misgivings. The unusual metrical structure of the poem reproduces precisely the equally unusual metrical structure of a very famous Welsh hymn whose first lines are, "Braint, braint/ Yw cael cymdeithas gyda'r saint". It is clearly not coincidental that this is a hymn about the communion of saints! The repetition of "Gwyn, gwyn" clearly replicates the repetition of "Braint, braint", something which is entirely destroyed by rendering "Gwyn, gwyn" as "Very holy". Furthermore, in the third line, the word "nef" means, not "sky" but "heaven", and the verb "mynnu", of which "myn" is a part, means "to insist". It wasn't the sky that called the snowdrops from the earth, it was heaven which insisted that they should rise. In the fourth line, even more crucially, the verb "prynu" doesn't so much mean "win" as "purchase" and it was a verb specifically and frequently used by Calvinistic Methodist preachers and theologians in particular to refer to Christ's ransom for many; "Y Brynedigaeth" was the purchase of mankind made by the sacrifice on the Cross. I do not think, in all honesty, that this connotation of "Golau a'u pryn o'u gwely pridd" can be gainsaid.

I note all this in regard to one brief translation not to diminish in any way Tony Conran's huge achievement as a translator, but simply to emphasise that the remarkable standards of faithfulness to the original that prevail in the Penguin book do not happen by chance, or even by intuition; they are the result of high craftsmanship and meticulous attention to detail which can often go unnoticed and which even the finest translators may not always apply.

The truth is that Tony Conran's work as a translator has been integral to his poetic career and that what he experienced in coming to terms with the great medieval poets has informed the remainder of his work in all kinds of ways. At the same time, he performed an immeasurable service to those of us who write in Welsh; whatever his explicitly stated motives, he has in fact brought the rich diversity of Welsh poetry to the attention of the outside world more faithfully and more fully than it had ever been done before, bringing to the task a huge commitment informed by a formidable intellect.

It may be allowable, in a contribution to a personal volume, to end on a personal note. I have known Tony since college days and have valued his friendship. I have known him as a good and forthright man who has lived his life with great courage. But I am not surprised that he is so fond of Dafydd ap Gwilym, because he shares that poet's wicked wit and mischievous, brave and unpredictable sense of humour; one of the finest things about knowing Tony is that when one comes across him, one's meetings almost always end in hilarity .

A Tribute to Old Delight
Les A. Murray

When Anthony Conran's *Penguin Book of Welsh Verse* came out in 1967, I was living in Penarth and exploring Wales and nearby southern England in my green Cortina. On an earlier visit to Britain, I had made some close friendships in Cardiff, and had been captivated by Wales. It was natural that when I got a chance to embark on that poor man's Grand Tour which tens of thousands of young Australians had started making in those still-affluent times I would gravitate first to Wales; there were things about the country which I wanted to understand, and a mood of national cultural revival was in the air, seemingly reversing the usual sad story of Celtic decline. A personal preparation for my amazed delight in Conran's pioneering Penguin book, and its importance in the development of my own writing, was that I had already begun feeling my way into the poetic traditions of a Celtic sister-culture, that of my own remote Gaelic forebears, and had at least got a bit beyond the coarser misinterpretations of that slippery term 'bardic'. This wasn't entirely ancestor-worship on my part, because Gaelic lay at least three centuries behind me, in my paternal descent. The Old Murrays had been Borderers for a couple of centuries, between being Highlanders and becoming Australians. I had been badly stymied, though, by uncertainty about proper Gaelic pronunciation: well-trained teachers were hard to find in Australia, and the orthography, even in modern Irish, can be nearly as misleading to the novice as that of English. The clear phonetic orthography of Welsh allowed me to sound the language and pronounce it with an accuracy which native judges approved, once I had sorted out the important difference, well explained in all its metrical implications in Conran's new edition, between penultimate stress and that tonic accent which marks final syllables and gives words their well-defined boundaries. Although Conran's Penguin book didn't have facing page texts in the original Welsh, the sheer quality and verbal music of his translations would become my highroad into the all-important formal side of Celtic poetry, and the basis of any understanding of this which I would attain.

I had read a lot of translations, and a lot of original texts in languages I knew well enough, but I had never seen translations as brilliant and immediately convincing as Conran's. Accurate or not, they were poetry of a high order in themselves, and reflected a tradition that was clearly of major importance. In all the years since that Penguin book came out, I have never again struck translations of poetry with so powerful an effect: Conran's versions of Welsh classical poems remain a unique memory for me. I have since seen translations by other hands of some of the same poems, and none has moved me in any comparable way. I have been moved by some translations of Irish and Scottish Gaelic poetry, but sadly never to the same extent: I still don't get enough of the music from them which I know must be there, and I haven't mastered Gaelic well enough to extract all the music for myself. For that, I'd probably have to develop a native ear, or something close to it. For Welsh (though this is something I obviously can't check directly upon) I have the impression Tony Conran developed one for me, and shared it fully with all his readers. Friends of mine in Wales told me when the book came out that it was a revelation to some of them too.

The effect of that Penguin book was bodily. The poetry clung in the ear, but it also went through the mind to the body's realm of dance and gesture. It did the same things to me as the poetry of

55

Fr. Hopkins S.J., whose work had turned me on to poetry itself when I was a schoolboy, and it did them from the same authoritative source. I had seen the isthmian canal of Hopkins' verse, and its excitingly difficult locks: now I was getting a sense of the aural ocean that had moved behind it. I was also imbibing a lasting corrective, ultimately beyond the grasp or at least beyond the traditions of my own language, but important as an ideal-absolute case, to the slackness of the *vers libre* and *vers libéré* which had pretty well taken over modern poetry in English. I began to see that as an intellectual's poetry, dependent on the aesthetics of interest. Poetry, in its fullness, requires more than that iconic quality which a text begins to have when conscious and unconscious thinking are brought into concert with each other; it also requires the sympathy of the body, the ghostly activation of ear and breath and muscles. When thought and dream harmonize with the element of gesture, of the dance, poetry becomes what I call Wholespeak, an utterance of the whole person, capable of addressing the wholeness of the person who receives it. Compared with this, most other utterance is Narrowspeak, of a lesser fullness which merely administers the world. And which may be needed, and indeed exist, mainly to regulate the excesses which poetry can bring in its train. This may be the real meaning of administration, to buffer poetry, or at least to counter-balance the iconic when it comes seeking embodiment.

Another aspect of Welsh classical poetry which worked powerfully on me through Conran's translations was a sense of ramified chiasmus, though I certainly didn't know that term back then. Chiasmus, for those who share my slackness about learning the names of technical poetic devices, is derived from the Greek letter chi(X) and really means cross-linkage, X-ing things together. John Hollander's excellent 1981 primer *Rhyme's Reason: A Guide to English Verse* gives several examples. One, not a verbal-musical one but one which works intellectually, is his line *Speech which in part reflects on parts of speech.* What echoed continually and fascinatingly for me out of Conran's translations of Welsh classical verse was an all-over patterning of cross reference and cross resonance, a kind of ever-growing crystal lattice of sound and sense at once. I was amazed by the continual fine shifts of key, of vowel colour, by how a sequence of consonants would appear with dark vowels between them, then immediately recur with an infilling of light vowels, like shadow and sunlight chasing each other across a rippling current. It was a powerful, ever-recurring mantra against randomness and chaos, this rapid miming of complex inter-relatedness, and it gave me the fascination with chiasmus that has been a feature of my own writing ever since. I don't think my continuing passion for masculine-feminine rhyme (fence/patience, fluttered/bird) arose precisely from Conran's Penguin book, since I had already encountered it in Gaelic poetry I had read; the Penguin book did, however, immensely sharpen my appreciation of it as a tripping, leaping, sometimes even limping alternative to the stiffer march of English rhyme, with its ever-successive finalities, its continual stoppage. I saw that rhyme, in the hands of its inventors and first masters, was a more flexible, resourceful thing than I had imagined, and capable of more nuance.

Equally, I was struck by the almost *cloisonée* quality of images and epithets in the older verse, the way they were packed tightly into the tense lacing of the verse, or displayed like quarterings in a complex heraldry:

> Son of Gruffudd, valor in battle,
> Your violence long, dragon of Ewias,
> For your fullness of rank, I praise you.
> Everyone praises you, kingdom's head!

57

I notice this heraldic imagery has been reflected in the new jacket design of Conran's anthology, where the original Penguin book carried an equally native and suggestive imagery of fitted stone walling. Beyond these impressions, as much visceral as intellectual, Conran's Penguin book gave me the delight of discovering a whole ancient and in the full sense classical tradition. For that, I needed the help of a detailed introduction, and the one he gave did not seem overlong to me. In a book of contemporary verse from one's own culture, too much prose guidance can be obtrusive and schoolmasterly, muffling the impact of the poetry itself, but with a survey of an unfamiliar literature or period, guidance isn't out of place. Also, Conran very tactfully kept the prose parts of his book separate from the poetry. The lecture ceased when we entered the gallery to view the works of art. In this, he constructed his book more wisely than most of the editors of that deservedly popular Penguin series. For example, one wasn't, while reading the poems, obliged to think about the problem, for modern anti-aristocratic tastes, of a poetry based for hundreds of years on eulogy and elegy addressed to warrior over-lords.

It is possible that Anthony (now Tony) Conran worries at this matter a bit too much, in the 1986 version of that splendid 1967 anthology. All poetry in all periods is substantially in hock to the class and sensibility which gives it patronage and a focus; the point doesn't need to be laboured. In our age, much good and nearly all mediocre poetry which gets published is obedient to the class sensibility of secularising university intellectuals, and deviates from their expected attitudes only gingerly or for deliberately naughty effect. What matters more is how far beyond what we may call the commissioning class a poetry may spread, and how freely poets elaborate their own art, either on their own or within some sort of poetic guild-tradition powerful enough to contain and refine the iconic needs of both their sponsors and of any wider public there may be beyond the sponsors. The old bards of Wales must have built their tradition well, for poetry to remain so strong a feature of Welsh life for centuries after the defection of the native lords who once upheld it. As Conran wrote in the Introduction to the Penguin book:

> The Welsh poet is still a leader in his community, a national figure who appears at public functons and is constantly called upon to give his opinions on questions of the day. He is therefore able to talk, in his poetry, of political matters (and even international affairs) with the certainty that a lot of influential people are going to listen. No English poet has been able to do this since Tennyson.

I can't seem to find that passage repeated in the 1986 rescension of his book. It did interest me very strongly in 1967, though, as a model for something which sporadically did happen in my own society and might be developed further. British readers sometimes profess a rather patronising scepticism when I tell them how influential poetry can at times be in Australia, and what a broad readership the best of it can attain, proportional to our population. Verse is also a medium which many Australians have always reached for to express things about their society; a strong current of 'light' newspaper verse overlapped with the evolving ballad tradition right through the nineteenth century and well into this one, and was a powerful former of attitudes. This verse was protected from the deadening conventions of contemporary High Art verse by the very fact of being regarded as light verse, and had a vastly wider readership than the stiff formalities of most of our early academic poets. Indeed, the coming of Modernism had the effect of killing off the real modernity of that tradition, at least in great part, and channelling it into academic obedience, though it sometimes reappears, as for example in the work of an excellent poet like Bruce Dawe. A rather ghastly parody of poets' influence is played out, here as elsewhere, when poets are invited to lend their name and pen to designated Left Wing causes in return for good reviews and freedom from harrassment at festivals, but that is the academy militant, a hangover from the Vietnam War period, and may pass away with that generation. Getting right away from the situation, and the generation I am caught up in, it seemed clear to me, in Wales two decades ago, that the noble courts and the eisteddfodau of Wales had created and preserved a highly trained public for poetry, a model for what might be created again.

The new rescension of Conran's anthology contains a good deal more explanatory prose, and I'm frank to admit that I need all the additional data too. The wholly new Appendix on Welsh metrics is particularly welcome, and is as easy to follow, probably, as a treatise on so intricate a matter could ever be. Having said this, though, the proportion of explanatory prose to poetry does now seem high; the cliffs do beetle a bit, and threaten to fall in on the stream as it glitters on its way. I may be imagining things, too, but the prose itself now seems a shade heavier and fussier, despite the brilliance of the many fine historical and stylistic distinctions it draws. I wonder if this is not in part a result of the great disappointment of St David's Day, 1979, when the voters of Wales, for their own reasons, knocked down a whole heap of clangorous furniture in the path of their own independence just as it seemed about to reach a measure of consummation. It's very presumptuous of an outsider even to mention these things, but I remember with some nostalgia that sunny hopeful mood that seemed to be abroad in Wales twenty years ago when I lived there. The right to plead in Welsh in the courts had not long been conceded, personal documents could be in Welsh or English, the Red Dragon was visible on public offices everywhere, Anglophone students in Cardiff were starting to attend Welsh-language classes – now when I go back to see my friends, much seems sadder, more dour, more embattled. Perhaps an outsider can be forgiven if he mistook a sectional revival for a national one, and mistook hope and energy for portents of a real shift in the deep mood of a society not his own. The emergence of the language into a modern sort of visibility may have been the consummation, rather than the national independence it seemed to presage.

If the updated version of Conran's anthology has a touch more of the museum about it, and a little less of the atmosphere of an exciting exhibition in a newly opened gallery, perhaps I should remember that its editor and I are both a couple of decades older now, and point out that the exhibition has been augmented by some excellent new work, particularly by women poets. In particular, I am bowled over by the work of Ann Griffiths (1776-1805). Even on a small sampling from a small output, she seems to have been a mystical poet worthy of at least some comparison with St John of the Cross. Again, if I was fascinated twenty years ago by the Welsh classical styles, and drew most from them, I was well aware even then that there were some modern poets of world importance in Welsh too. I am happy to see more of both Saunders Lewis and David Gwenallt Jones in the updated edition, just as I have been happy, in both editions, to note an absence of that freezing condescension towards religion and religious poetry so common in present-day scholarly books. It is a pity, though, that the book has changed publishers, and lost the world-wide Penguin distribution. Even if I had not been living in Wales twenty years ago, at exactly the right time and place for Conran's translations to come into my hands, I would have bought the original Penguin book and been knocked sideways by it; I suspect that its effect on me would still have been profound, even if I hadn't been able to track down so many of its allusions in my battered green Cortina. On the other hand, we never see

Poetry Wales Press books in Australia unless we somehow learn of their existence and order them specially; I wouldn't have seen the updated edition if I had not been asked to write this memoir-review of it. I hope this isn't a symptomatic shrinkage of the Welsh presence in the wider world, for the essence of so ancient and brilliant a poetic tradition deserves to be kept before readers everywhere.

One Harbour Light
Steve Griffiths

Tony Conran is a known and valued friend, now. He began as an unseen friend as the distances grew and strained between me and the places that made me. I was always a cultural hybrid, my father from an old family ranged between Llangollen and Llandudno, but born in Belfast - and not present after I was four; my mother from the Wirral, a young mother evacuated to Bala in the war, lonely and ready to run away with my father to Anglesey, and then rather associating Wales with her downfall and pointing her boys to a nice English university which would somehow reverse that downfall, with that absolute faith in the power of education that so distinguished the 'fifties from these days. And so to Cambridge and beyond, without much of a look back: much of the excitement about poetry was focused on Europe, Rimbaud, Rilke, Herbert, Holub, Vozhnesensky, Yevtushenko. I didn't think much about what I had brought with me: R.S.Thomas and Dylan Thomas pretty deeply ingrained already, the latter an influence I was already working to escape from at nineteen; unacknowledged memories that I had been singing the words of Pantycelyn and Ann Griffiths all my life, miraculously managing not to speak Welsh at school in Amlwch, I think at least partly due to the tough experience of my mother as a single parent that set us apart in the Wales of the 'fifties; and a deep rooting in the landscapes I grew up in, which has been growing and developing into other attachments ever since.

In spite of the support of a couple of teachers at Amlwch, and the early encouragement of Roland Mathias, as far as poetry was concerned I was a pretty isolated autodidact. Cambridge enriched and disorientated. I brought with me the Gwyn Jones and Thomas Jones translation of *The Mabinogion*. And then I stumbled on Tony Conran's *Penguin Book of Welsh Verse*, in a state of sublime ignorance. There was so much in this bridge back that I immediately recognised. It's a shock to go back over the book and realise how many connections and seeds there were that have become part of my poetic landscape.

Two qualities that struck me immediately were the harsh and the erotic. The harsh was in the oldest poems, Taliesin and Aneirin, and connected with the rock I knew, with the harshness of R.S. Thomas, and with the strength of Basil Bunting's *Briggflatts* which harks back explicitly to Aneirin. It is a harshness in Tony's translations that is tempered with the tragedy in detail, the hesitations in slaughter. How much is there for a poet to learn from these lines?

> Breathless before a girl, he paid for his mead.
> His shield boss is broken. Hearing the warcry
> He gave no quarter to those that he hounded.

Here is a tension between inner vulnerability and public violence that Tony was to apply magnificently in his own poem to the Falklands dead. There is a spring in the line which demands attention, not only from the alliteration that echoes *cynghanedd*, but the monsyllables that prepare the ground for the clang of 'breathless.... broken....hearing....hounded....warcry....quarter'.

Such an ear helped to remind me, with time, where I belonged whether I wanted to or not.

Reading the translations also meant a ritual naming of places I knew intimately: the killing of Hywel ab Owain Gwynedd above

Pentraeth, Cemais in the Cantref of Talybolion, and Gwalchmai ap Meilyr exalting Owain Gwynedd, before whom:

> .... ran a miserable confusion,
> Ruin and battle and a grievous end -
> On struggle, blood and struggle; on terror, dire terror;
> And a thousand war-shouts about Tal y Moelfre

Here was a poetry out of the villages my schoolfriends came from, which checked me in my trajectory outward. It was shockingly not Cambridge or Paris. It began to suggest, at great distance, the possibility of a poetry of place. In Anglesey, among the gentle greens and intimate tricklings, there is a darkness and a sense of loss, and thus something deceptive in its enticement that the translations begin to explain. It is all the more tantalising because there are so few physical remains and artefacts. In Wales, the continuity has to be all in the head and in the clues of the landscape, which is why the language is so important.

There was a different kind of validation in the sex, for example in Hywel ab Owain Gwynedd and Dafydd ap Gwilym: and in the case of the former I hesitate to use the word 'sensuality'. In "Hywel's Boast of Women" I recognised the boasts of my teenage male contemporaries, more commonly wishful thinking in Amlwch as I remember it, and only slightly more delicately put in the unreconstructed Cambridge of the late sixties. Such empty-headed boasting had been given a voice eight hundred years before in Gwynedd, giving lust a context. So this was something poetry could do too:

> I had a girl of the same mind one day;
> I had two, their praise is greater;
> I had three and four, and fortune.

Once again, Tony Conran was laying trails forwards and backwards for me, allowing an access which was the direct heritage of others, and a dislocated one for me that kept getting up and hitting me. One of the anthology's trails leads forward from that *droit de seigneur* to the uncovering of the voice of lustful women through Dafydd Johnston's excellent anthology, *Mediaeval Welsh Erotic Poetry*, and reflects the social changes, embodied in personal lives, of the last thirty years.

With Dafydd ap Gwilym, there is a joy in self-deprecation, with a freshness and clarity that Tony gives us like the slap of a wet fish:

> That pale and flirt-faced lad
> With hair from his sister's head -
> Adulterous must be the gaze
> Of a fellow with such ways.

This was important, because to say that I was uneasy as a teenager with what I saw as the slate-grey surfaces of Welsh Nonconformism would be an understatement. I could see myself growing up in Amlwch through these poems in another, more accepting, light. It is easy to see where some self-deprecating lines among green foliage in my first book, *Anglesey Material*, came from. The self-deprecation - the onset of maturity in learning to chuckle occasionally at yourself and your failures - are part of what Tony calls the 'anti-images' of the classical period of Welsh poetry:

> Instead of the lord, there is the outlaw, the thief, the
> outcast; instead of the house, there is the glade in the
> birchwoods, or sometimes, even more explicit, the hut
> that the poet has made there, where he hopes his lady-
> love will tryst with him ....

This is an essentially subversive strand, with an energy that perhaps mirrors, as Tony suggests, a loss of solid political aspiration
following military defeat. It continues to run with political defeat:
but Dafydd ap Gwilym remains its summit, if subversion can
have a summit - I have written somewhere about 'the mountains
upturned':

> God's not so fierce, my friend,
> As you old men pretend,
> Nor would He damn the soul
> For woman loved, nor girl.

I too was interested in denying the ferocity of God, and took
much pleasure in this translation. But the ultimate celebration of
the outcast's thwarted desire is in Dafydd ap Gwilym's rumbus-
tious downfall in a tavern, with a certain amount of political edge
added to the alarums of a loud brass cauldron:

> 'There's a Welshman on the prowl!'
> - Oh hot ferment of betrayal -
> 'He'll rob us, if we let him!
> Look out you're not the victim' ....
>
> I stood, in the foul havoc
> Of rage, silent in the dark; ....
> I found my own bed safe and sure
> Though without sleep or treasure,
> Thank the Saints, freed of distress.
> I ask now God's forgiveness.

As a narrative, this is a *tour de force*, yet it is multi-dimensional: it
has a profundity with the lightest of touches. In the humour
there is always a great generosity of spirit. And that last, conven-

67

tional line is charged with a tongue in the cheek so large one can only wonder about the sexual practices of the time - yet a sincerity, and a gratitude for self-preservation, though left with neither "sleep nor treasure". Dafydd ap Gwilym has qualities that are entirely contemporary, and Tony conveys them, though in some places I have difficulties with his poetic inversions for the sake of rhyme.

Re-reading Tony Conran's Introduction to the anthology gave me shock after shock of recognition. It has borne the years extremely well - or have I grown into it? It is extraordinarily comprehensive not only in its literary grasp, but in its socio-historical sweep, made all the more effective by his confidence as a critic of contemporary culture and its losses. It reminds me of Tony's immense influence as a teacher - and even in London I meet English students of his from twenty-five years ago who remember him as something special. In retrospect, it puts him in a light I had not thought of, as a critic with the cross-disciplinary, integrating purpose of a Raymond Williams or the then new historians like E.P. Thompson. But within that context there is a driving poetic vision, that begins with the "magical content of Welsh poetry" with origins in "primitive Indo-European magic concerning the making of kings":

> Much of the intentional obscurity of Welsh poetry springs from this magical origin. The spell, as an art-form, is not ususally conducive to sweetness and light.

This may have been just what I wanted to hear, with a head full of magic pulled by osmosis from the hut circles at South Stack and the transformations of light on the sea - and a head full of early Dylan Thomas. The Gnomic Stanzas, so dear to Nigel Jenkins, were certainly what I wanted to hear, in this expression of mystery and paradox, given in Tony's translations in a barbed and worldly way that give us a kind of Welsh hybrid of Tao Te Ching and *haiku*. Is there anything like it in the British Isles?

> Mountain snow, red feet of hens;
> Where it chatters, water's but shallow;
> Big words add to any disgrace ....

> Mountain snow, white house-roofs;
> If tongue were to tell what the heart may know
> Nobody would be neighbours ....

> Mountain snow, day has come;
> Every sad man sick, half-naked the poor;
> Every time, a fool gets hurt.

These stanzas have a weight that can serve as a model for any poet, because again they bear it so lightly, with the distillation of folk-wisdom. It's a wisdom that expresses a moment of clarity, that then turns back on itself and embodies paradox. This points forward across the years like an arrow to R.S.Thomas, and I too recognise that process.

In his description of the place of the "magical element", Tony Conran suggests a dynamic in the process of writing which has preoccupied me for years:

> .... Welsh poetry is at its most civilized and mature
> whenever conditions enabled the poets to transcend
> the magical element most completely. Transcend,
> please note, not forget or discard ....

At the time I read this, I was much preoccupied with the difficulty of my own very inward-looking work, and with the problem,

69

and seduction, of the difficulty of early Dylan Thomas; and I saw the movement of Yeats, from complexity to a simplicity that has clearly been worked for, as the gameplan of every poet. There was no metropolitan urbanity in this view. I think I see from re-reading Tony's Introduction how much this is a question of getting the right balance of the private (which may contain highly charged imaginative material which may have individualistic origins, but has parallels with what Tony describes as a tribal poetic experience) and the public, which is a kind of movement towards maturity without losing the magical, or childhood, element, and which in some way traces the course of the development of early Welsh poetry towards its classical flowering. It's a vision that can integrate the very personal in a wider culture that has a long tradition in Wales. It is no coincidence that Tony discusses the bourgeoisie's distrust of ritual, and that he has throughout his life directed his own poems as gifts to those he loves: the poem as a personal and ritual act of generosity, or response to generosity. I can think of no greater recognition that I can give personally to Tony's work than my increasing movement towards that view of poetry, which makes all kinds of psychological and social sense. Recently, the daughter of a friend of mine was suffering from depression. She had also been studying Philip Larkin for 'A' Level. We discussed this, and agreed that she needed to read Philip Larkin like she needed a hole in the head. Poetry can be a gift; it is one way of respecting the activity itself; and if it helps us to work towards maturity, generosity of spirit, a moment of enlightenment, then Tony Conran has given non-Welsh-speakers a route-map that's as clear and rewarding as it was nearly thirty years ago when I found it in the bewilderment of my late teens.

Working with the Translator
Menna Elfyn

Most poets, in one sense or another, are late developers - Tony Conran excepted! It was certainly very late in the day when I got to know Tony, but I've tried to make up for all those lost moments in the last few years. It was in my teenage days that I first discovered Tony Conran, in a bookshop in Carmarthen, in the form of the *Penguin Book of Welsh Verse* - a find of considerable importance in that it prompted me to read Welsh-language poetry. It is indeed ironic that I, a Welsh-speaker, should have come across Welsh poetry first of all in English, but that early stimulation was every bit as exciting as the language activism in which I was engaged at the time. Yet why, I remember wondering, had this person chosen to involve himself in Welsh poetry? I can still recall parts of that fine Introduction, and I continue to be amazed at his ability to invoke intricate concepts and ideas in such a matter-of-fact style. Who was this Tony Conran? Was he Welsh? Did he live in Wales, or was he simply offering Welsh poetry outward as a curiosity for the English-speaking world?

Now, in the 'nineties, those ill-thought responses seem so silly (a favourite Conran word, by the way). But at the time he seemed an enigma. I caught sight of the occasional Conran poem, the odd book. He seemed, from what I read, to be involved in Welsh life, but where was he? Was he in hiding? Was he a recluse? Poets in Wales tend to be visible creatures, many indeed, like myself, more visible than one would wish. There's a certain inevitability, if you're a Welsh poet, that you will rub

shoulders, queuing for a milkshake at the Eisteddfod or performing poetry in support of some cause, with others of your kind.

It was just such an event that got me thinking a little more
about Conran the man. Nigel Jenkins and I had undertaken to
produce a volume of peace poems, *Glas-Nos*, for CND Cymru
in 1987, to mark the fifth birthday of 'Nuclear Free Wales'. High
on Nigel's list of poets was Tony Conran, and the poem he submitted, "Research", was a powerful and sensitive gem:

> Those intelligent young men in the Ukraine
> Would, if we met, show me photos
> Of round-eyed daughters. They have nightmares ...

I became an instant Tony Conran fan. But wait, there was more:
accompanying the poem was a translation in Welsh by Gwyn
Thomas. We had asked only for a poem of his in English but
Tony, respecting the bilingual nature of the book, had sent versions in both English and Welsh.

The book launch at the Oakley Arms in Maentwrog was a lively
affair; the place was full of CND campaigners many of whom
had brought food and refreshments for a bumper night of celebration. I remember wondering to myself when I heard Tony's
wife Lesley read "Research" why he wasn't at the launch himself,
and on the drive home I voiced puzzlement that I thought I'd
seen his handwriting, even scrawlier than mine, on a copy of
Glas-Nos that had been raffled that night. "But Menna," said the
driver in some bewilderment, "you were sitting right next to
him." An opportunity lost ...

Eventually, however, we did meet, albeit somewhat fleetingly -
when Cymru-Cuba held an event to welcome the poet Eliseo
Diego to Wales; and I heard a reading of his poem "A Square of
Grey Slate" which was presented to the poet Pedro Pérez Sarduy

at the Cymru-Cuba Resource Centre at the National Eisteddfod in Rhyl in 1985.

It was during a conference at Gregynog, at a time when my readings outside Wales were increasing in number, and organisers were pressing me for English translations, that Tony mentioned that he had tried translating my poetry but had given up. What was it about my work, I wondered, that was so untranslatable? The years passed by, and I turned for those translations to other poet friends.

The next time I met Tony was when he received the 1993 BBC Arts Award nomination for *Castles*, a collection whose sheer vibrancy and word power impressed me hugely. Later that year I discovered that it was Tony who had read my bilingual volume *Eucalyptus* for the Arts Council, to whom Gomer had submitted it for a production grant. He had commended it highly, but questioned the ability of one of the translators. One person's translations seemed not to be worthy of the poet: they turned out to be mine! Tony offered his assistance, and our writer/translator relationship began.

I wasn't quite sure what to expect. After all, it's not so easy to open one's heart and mind to a relative stranger. My poet friends, as translators of my work, knew me well enough to get on with the job. This, however, was hard work.

Tony's letters arrived in my house like gift poems, as rich in their way as Dafydd ap Gwilym's. They were like seagulls, demanding flight, alighting on waves of thought ... Here are some edited highlights.

> Now for a few minor [sic!] points. In "Coch yr Aeron" you translate *cloddion* as 'hedgerows', don't you? That conjures up a very civilized countryside to me, quite different to the squelchy moorland where they grow - as your poem makes clear and as I've found them in

73

the hollows on a Norwegian *fjellsied*. A *clawdd* seems
to have been originally the earth thrown up when you
dig a trench - hence its three main meanings, a ditch,
an earthwork and some kind of boundary like a hedge.
How do you use the word normally? In my translation
I've played safe and used 'Behind hedgebanks and
dykes' - the banks suggested by your *'aeliau'r cloddion'*
and by the kind of rubble-cum-earthwork banks, with
a ragged thorn hedge on top, that you often find lining
the roads on Welsh moors. Dykes - like *cloddion* - is
ambiguous - it can mean an earthwork - Offa's Dyke -
or it can mean a trench or ditch.

These were questions which I hadn't even considered when I
translated this poem, "Cranberries", for a Poetry Society anthology published by Hutchinson in 1990. Tony admitted to great
difficulties with my use of words not found in the dictionary.
The phone would ring and there would be Lesley asking on
Tony's behalf for clarification as to what precisely I meant by a
certain phrase. His impatience was that of a sculptor interrupted
in the middle of his work, with his materials cracking under the
weight of the drive for perfection.

There were occasions when I felt guilty to be taking up his time
when he should have been concentrating on his own work. I was
all too aware of the meagre financial recompense normally
offered for this kind of work. His reply to my concern was typical of his nature:

I'm a rather feudal sort of bloke, and would have been
quite content if you had just given me your favour to
wear in tournaments and battles and things like that ...
What worries me is that you'll be dismayed by my
excessiveness.

There *were* disagreements. Once or twice I had to argue my case. There were truces, cease-fires, negotiated agreements on words here and there - that added spice to the work and increased, letter by letter, my admiration for the man. There are those who will shy away from challenging a feminist - proof, it seems to me, that they do not genuinely believe in equality. Tony never once presumed that we were on anything other than equal ground, and because of that we were able to engage, when necessary, in a healthy power struggle. He scolded me once when, making some weak attempt to score a point, I said "but literature is all about generosity, don't you think?" "Not," he protested, "when it interferes with your critical judgement." Another round lost, hands down.

Once or twice we got into an argument about the use of a single word. In "Cranberries" I wanted 'blush', he wanted 'redden'. He wrote to me:

> If for some reason that I can't quite see, you still think blush is better then redden ... , it will fit sonically all right. Change it in your text, if you want ... But redden still seems better to me!

I settled for 'redden'.

In another letter he stated:

> The only thing is, translating is not a job I can do for more than a week or so at a time at full pressure without a kind of weariness taking over. Also, I'm unsure of how you are responding, and I have moments of doubt whether you'd want me to go on in this bull-in-a-china-shop sort of way.

To think of Conran getting weary made me smile. Although not known for my lack of stamina, I could hardly keep the ball in the court. As thrilled as I was with his professionalism and commitment, those letters, not to mention his probing questions, could sometimes render me breathless. Another statement he made demonstrates the depth of his involvement with the work of transcreation:

> Trouble is, one gets so intimate with the poet one is translating, it is a bit difficult to draw the line. By all means tell me where to get off.

Tony Conran, a soul-mate whose values I share and admire, is no longer, to me, an enigma, though he may still be so to others, for he is not the easy-to-know poet-about-the-Eisteddfod kind of literary figure. The 'cost of his strangeness' is at the very heart of his passion and his Welshness. He surely has no rival for the passionate attention he devotes to the two languages, and his belief in their equal validity. There has been much talk in the 'nineties about the renaissance of Welsh prose writing. It could be argued that Tony gave Welsh poetry a sense of renaissance at a crucial moment in the Welsh language revivalism of the 'sixties. Perhaps the time will come when Welsh-language poetry goes out into the world and declares its freedom; and perhaps the richness of English writing in Wales, alongside her, will also claim recognition. In such a moment, Tony Conran will be seen as the Bendigeidfran of verse, armed not with a spear but a steely sense of urgency.

For Tony C.
Raymond Garlick

The first thing I ever heard you say
Opened a window on Wordsworth
For me - and you were still a student
Then.

      Since then you've built a clerestory
For us in the Welsh basilica,
In whose light we see translation
Doesn't just benefit bishops.

Critic, poet, scholar, it's not
These in the end my pencil rings,
But the raging life-force in you,
That consumes, and argues, and sings.

"Shaman of shifting form":
Tony Conran and Welsh *barddas*
M.Wynn Thomas

From the very beginning, Tony Conran's translation of Welsh poetry was an integral aspect of his own development as a poet, so that throughout his career there has been a symbiotic relationship between the two activities.[1] One way he himself has offered of accounting for this is to see it as characteristic of his generation. According to Conran, the English-language writers emerging in Wales during the 'fifties were culturally disorientated:

> Like many Anglo-Welsh poets of the second generation - John Tripp, myself, Meic Stephens, Gillian Clarke - [Bobi Jones'] adult experience was of post-Depression Wales. For older people, and poets among them, it had often seemed that the only thing to do with Wales was to leave it .... But now a new generation was coming to be aware of what we had lost .... For most of us Wales was a journey into an exile we were born with. We were heirs to a richness we could only apprehend as memories of childhood. We were third-generation immigrants into our own land, easier with English people, very often, than with our still Welsh-speaking compatriots. Threatened by both the ruling-class English intelligentsia we were trained to serve, and by the native Welsh culture that we felt had the birthright, we tried to make room for ourselves.

> We wrote elegies for lost Wales. We proclaimed that
> the Dragon has two tongues. We translated Welsh
> poetry.[2]

In this passage many of Conran's leading themes and preoccupations are brought together to form a highly suggestive profile of the circumstances underlying important features of his poetic practice. The condition of exile is touched upon in all its complexity   if early exile in England helped Conran rediscover and focus his Welshness, then the returnee's experience of a second exile, this time in his very 'own' country, helps us see his poetry 'from the Welsh' (in several senses of that phrase) as a second kind of homecoming, a journey out of the exile he was born with. This 'journey' may, in turn, be alternatively imaged as anamnaesis, a restoration of lost memory. In a recent review, Conran chided Leslie Norris for his insouciant discarding of the historical ties that result in social commitments, and referred with approval to a famous contrasting Irish case: "[Patrick] Kavanagh did take responsibility for his past, as far as lay in him as a poet. 'The Great Hunger' alters the way we look at people now, not simply laments what has passed."[3]

So, really "to take responsibility for [the] past" means an "alter[ation in] the way we look at people now". "If one can really penetrate the life of another age", T.S. Eliot approvingly observed of Ezra Pound the translator, "one is penetrating the life of one's own."[4] Such perceptions go to the very heart of Conran's practice: they alert us to the politics of Conran's poetics of translation, and help us see how his own English-language poetry uses a new counter-cultural syntax, and a grammar of alternative social relationship, derived, courtesy of Welsh-language poetry, from his country's past. Indeed, it could be said that in Welsh-language poetry Conran found a 'form' of social vision that, by precisely focussing his own radical dissatisfactions with the contemporary world, progressively saved him, as a poet, from dissipating such feelings in mere romantic nostalgia ("the Fifties were not much,/ Lacked the collective point of a great epoch")[5], and crudely dissenting anti-capitalist polemic.

Judging by his work, this was a very real temptation. The opening poem of his early collection *Spirit Level* depicts a world degenerated into violence and madness, but finds comfort in a Wagnerian image of a resolute dwarf, hidden in the crannies of a rock, hammering a sabre blade, and "wait[ing] his hero, unmindful all is lost."[6] Later, in *Life Fund*, Conran's anguish at the suicide in 1971 of his friend, the painter Brenda Chamberlain, finds expression in phrases of desperate crudeness: "Brenda, this death of yours,/ This acquiescence in the laws of the market/– How could you do it?"[7] Such recurring false notes – of sentimentally grandiose heroism and of bewildered shrillness – are poignant indications of the difficulty Conran may initially have experienced in addressing his own times. In the characteristically honest poem "No!" he confessed (although he would doubtless hate the term) that regret is "an old friend on my doorstep", spoke of "Nostalgia/ For the hand-made, the times before the last,/ Where every decorative thing had patina", admitted how easy it was to hate modern "domesticated vistas", and noted how "Paranoia/ For the thousandth time/ Threatens to kidnap me." The poem ends, however, on a courageous note of self-confrontation that seems also to mark the site of his best poetry: "No, I have to say,/ This is my century./ I shall not be abducted" (*LF*, 117). Paradoxically, his English-language modernisation of ancient Welsh-language poetry has been one of the crucial sociopoetic strategies that have saved him from being abducted by the past.

"We tried to make room for ourselves", wrote Conran of his generation in the passage quoted above, and much of his energy as a poetic *makker* has been invested in that undertaking. Even had the young Conran seriously wished to find room in 'English' literature it would have been denied him following the death in 1953 of Dylan Thomas, the "Don Quixote of the vaunted phrase" (*FP*, 42), since an anti-Welsh reaction ensued that succoured the anti-bardic wryness of such Sancho Panzas as the "prosemen" John Betjeman, Philip Larkin, and the Movement poets. "It was no time to inaugurate thought," he remarked in the Audenesque epitaph for the 'fifties written in 1958, "Only to entrench ambiguous positions,/ Afraid of feeling, afraid also of not feeling" (*FP*, 24). In the elegy that effectively marked Conran's poetic debut, Thomas was praised for establishing "A territory kept apart/ With cunning phrases" (*FP*, 42). But already the young poet knew better than to attempt to move into that newly vacated territory. An elegy, the older Conran was shrewdly to note, can be a way of drawing a line under a life, indicating the finality of closure.

Two years later, in 1955, he elegised a very different cultural figure, the Welsh poet R.Williams Parry, adopting (and adapting) for his purpose the mixed metres of the *awdl* form, so utterly foreign to English poetry, that had first brought Williams Parry his eisteddfodic fame. Ostensibly, Conran pays him the tribute of deference, in that the whole poem is organised around the trope of a difficult pilgrimage ("plodding where you were speedy") into the very heartland of Williams Parry's imagination: "For his love it was, we'd argue,/ This wistful, antiquated wood/ Where all the visions end/ And the hurt stabs out/ No more with vivid/ And desperate drums" (*FP*, 8). The Welsh poetry becomes a means whereby English-speakers may re-map their culture through recognising their own land anew: "And your wounds glinting/ Like frosty rivers/ That we always knew/ Ran through our land" (*FP*, 8). But coexisting with this genuine sense of indebtedness to Williams Parry (and therefore to the Welsh language and its literature) is the unspoken counterweight of pride in having

81

wrought in English a distinctive form answerable to indigenous Welsh experience, the pleasure of having found in Welsh a mode of writing that licences and underwrites an extravagance of language of a kind the English tradition (recoiling from Dylan Thomas) is busily deploring, and the triumph of having successfully engineered in English a "journey" into the very interior of Welsh literature, to claim what had seemed to be the exclusive "birthright" of "native Welsh culture." In other words, this Trojan Horse of an elegy is an important example of Conran making room for himself, as English-language writer, both "within" and "against" the Welsh-language tradition.

Of his generation of Welsh writers brought up in English, Conran finally reports: "We wrote elegies for lost Wales. We proclaimed that the Dragon has two tongues. We translated Welsh poetry." But one member of that generation, and one only, learned and internalised the Welsh language so completely that he became not only a distinguished Welsh scholar but also one of the leading Welsh-language poets of the post-war period. Bobi Jones' extraordinary achievement continues to fascinate Conran, who has accounted for it in terms that reveal him to be Jones' *alter ego*:

> If you want to be culturally born again, writing in what is not, for you, a wholly established language has a lot to recommend it .... The wastage is likely to be enormous .... But the possibility is there. What you lose in stylistic sureness you can gain in energy and innocence. From Dylan Thomas to Allen Ginsberg, from Idris Davies to Bobi Jones, this is the Devil's bargain that poets have been forced or delighted to strike (*BJ*, 69).

There are "striking" parallels here with Conran's own situation.

Although he has continued, of course, to write in English, he has deliberately used his limited mastery of Welsh (a reading knowledge, but no oral fluency), and his qualified familiarity with Welsh-language literature (he reputedly works as much from cribs supplied by others as by laboriously deciphering frequently difficult texts) to defamiliarise and destabilise the inherited norms of English expression. In that sense, and by those means, English has ceased to be for him "a wholly established language", his use of it having been informed, and re formed, by his translating experience. His, too, has been a Devil's bargain - the voluntary relinquishing of "stylistic sureness" for the uncertain promise of innovation and for the first two decades or so Conran's consistently adventurous poetry was accordingly of "strikingly" uneven quality. A constant throughout this impressive career in experimentation has been his interest in the combined ethical and creative power of otherness, and it is, perhaps, under this rubric that his dealings, as poet-translator, with Welsh poetry may be most rewardingly studied.

★   ★   ★

The need to nurture a care for, in the form of attention to, the other is the single most abiding feature of Conran's imagination. A failure to do so may result either in the solipsism he effectively portrays in his poem "Prospero's Dream" (*SL*, 72), or in the imperial, Urizenic, imagination whose appropriative gestures he dramatises through the arrangement of arrogant capital letters in "Space":

CLOCKWORK ETERNITIES UNWIND AS I PENETRATE.
I HAVE REACHED DEAD NEBULAE TO REASON WITH THIS KITTEN.
I TAME TO EQUABLE TEMPERAMENT THE MELISMA OF STARS.
            but the kitten in its own
            becoming space watches the sun

> sparkle, the leaf turn in the
> light air, leaves it turn,
> attends to the speckled light
> of its own otherwise space, cat
> in the green sunshine, its
> own becoming grace (*SL*, 78-79)[8]

At his best, Conran shows an ability, equal to his unremitting concern, to acknowledge the "own otherwise space" of animals, people - and cultures. How to relate to otherness without reducing it to sameness is a problem with which he can already be seen struggling in his earliest poetry. "I would have each act/ Definitive as an equation,/ Solved into mystery/ By an awareness of persons", he writes in "The Swan", as he courts a girl by respecting her freedom: "I would have you speak, Cordelia,/ Such love as you think fit/ Under no pressure of my pride/ Or your too covetous duty" (*SL*, 23). And in "Four Personae" - one of the earliest examples of his turn to Welsh poetry - he describes the poet Llywarch Hen's assumption of the voice of Heledd, to speak the great lines of mourning for the fall of the princely house of Cynddylan: "I/ Wondered if it was I that made them/ Or she for whom they were made./... Oddly surprised by the hallucination,/ That it was she, incarnate sorrow,/ That made the lamentings I made/ To mourn Cynddylan, her dead lord" (*FP*, 14). This sense of poetry as transactional, as a form of communication along the "axis" of I and Thou, and therefore as existing in a space between self and other, is, of course, one that Conran claims to have derived initially from Welsh poetry of the archaic period. Already in the 'fifties he was asserting that "the poetry of personal definition is as obsolete as Napoleon's battles" (*SL*, 77), and in his verse "Ars Poetica" he further asserted that "A third person poetry can no longer enact a civilisation. The poet cannot stabilize his art/in the tarnishing medium of I and IT" (*SL*, 80).

It is precisely this kind of concern with alterity that lies, or so

Wolfgang Iser has recently argued, at the heart of the best kind of translation:

> In this respect a foreign culture is not simply sub-
> sumed under one's own frame of reference; instead
> the very frame is subjected to alterations in order to
> accommodate what does not fit. Such changes run
> counter to the idea of one culture being superior to
> another, and hence translateability emerges as a
> counter-concept to cultural hegemony .... Translation
> of otherness is primarily concerned with giving it its
> due without subsuming it under preconceived notions
> .... Translateability, however, requires a discourse that
> allows the transposition of a foreign culture into one's
> own. Such a discourse has to negotiate the space
> between foreignness and familiarity[.][9]

A comment Conran made in an interview provides an interesting gloss on Iser's passage: "I translate for a wide variety of reasons, one being that I like making verses, and the technical problem involved in making English poems in so very unEnglish a way. And for a disabled person like myself, who has lived so much through other people's experience, to put such poetic expertise as I have at the service of other poets is not so strange."[10]

The arresting insights into Welsh poetry that have found expression through both Conran's translations and his commen-taries may be seen as deriving precisely from the poetry's inalienable otherness, the way in which it continues, in his expe-rience, to occupy a space "between foreignness and familiarity." In the interview cited above, for instance, he distinguished between his own versions of Welsh poetry and those of Gwyn Williams, whose *The Rent that's Due to Love* had first awakened his interest in translation: "why Gwyn's were complaisant about being used as cribs and mine are not may have been something to do with the fact that as a Welsh-speaker the originals were present to him in all their complexity and beauty before, during, and after the translating process, whereas to me they are discovered only in that process, and then dimly remembered afterwards"(12). As he further remarked, "I cannot see what is good in a Welsh poem until I have translated it into my own verse. My Welsh is so abysmally poor. I have to wrestle with a Welsh poem to see why it is a poem at all" (12). The point is surely crucial, since it helps explain why, as critic and translator, he is such a startlingly good inquisitor of structures (in Wallace Stevens' phrase), and why, as poet, he is such a correspondingly good artificer of structures. Rather like the magician Gwydion, as depicted in his recent verse drama *Blodeuwedd*, Conran is an inspired detective of mutating patterns and patterns of mutation, a "shaman of shifting form/ Huntsman of nuance and trickery."[11] His unerring eye for where the power of a poem really lies finds metaphoric expression in the recent poem "Wild Form", where he sets aside the hydrangea's ineffectual "florets" in order to uncover "the peppercorn buds [that] mean business —/ The real flowers/ Symmetrically accurate/ Jabs of power" (*B*, 12).

His best-known insights, of course, relate to his view that Welsh-language poetry of the great ages articulates, at the level of style, poetic convention and syntax, the deep structure of a form of "civilization" (no less) that is wholly "other" than that of England. A full consideration of this complex subject would involve a comparison of Conran with the many other modern poets of radically conservative persuasion, whose anti-capitalist animus has led them to romanticise past times (Eliot's "dissociation of sensibility"; Yeats' Cuchulainn; Pound's Confucius; Olson's Mayan civilization; Saunders Lewis's Catholic Europe of the Middle Ages; T. Gwynn Jones's Penmon). But as Conran's ideological reading of traditional Welsh praise (or boast) poetry, and the "gift" poems that reading underpins, are being addressed by other contributors to this volume, it seems sensible to note some of the additional ways in which Conran the poet has profited from the insights of Conran the translator. For instance, he realised as early as his first reading of Welsh poetry in translation, in *The Rent that's Due to Love*, that whereas in English poetry it was the vowel that coloured and energised saying, in Welsh the consonant was supreme. Thirty years later, in an essay on Hopkins, he drew a fascinating distinction between *cynghanedd* poetry as practised by the Gogynfeirdd (the poets of the princes) and by the later Cywyddwyr (the poets of the gentry). In the former case, he argued, consonantal repetition is primarily used "to decorate and pick out the stresses in the body of the line, before you get to the main rhyme ... It helps to isolate the stressed words".[12] The volume *Blodeuwedd*, that Conran published more or less contemporaneously with the Hopkins essay (1988), contains several examples of how he as poet had by then thoroughly internalised the lesson learned from the Welsh:

> The snow's gone, the green sinews
> Of the world stretch in the woods.
> Feeders of light come mewing
> Leaf puts its key in the lock. (*B*, 18)

It is a fine example of the analytical, critical, intelligence at work in Conran's mature poetry. Instead of attempting to reproduce in English the precise patterns of Welsh *cynghanedd*, he has penetrated to the very *raison d'être* of the early Welsh practice (alliteration as reinforcing stress) and has thus been able to make appropriately modified, powerfully functional, use of it in English.

In its own way, such a passage signifies a kind of otherness, since it occupies in English a space "between foreignness and familiarity." The same could be said about "Girl Pregnant":

Another being is at her gravity.
She is pulled to its purposes
Like a continent. Slowly, her flesh drifts.

Crops are re-distributed
As she passes through new climates.
Around her contours vineyards are turreted.

Sleepy volcanoes crouch in the haze of her.
She is well-watered. To the South
Deserts recede into mirage. (*B*, 16)

Such writing, vividly reminiscent of the poetry of Alan Llwyd or Bobi Jones, is, in Conran's terms, a "Platonic" poem; that is, it is a praise poem in celebration of the mystery of "fertility" ("pregnancy" being simply the *human* form of that phenomenon). The poem is a ritual of language in honour of that concept, a verbal fertility rite, and the point of ritual (as Conran has remarked) is that it is repeated because it has already been proved to be efficacious. In other words, like any ritual, this poem is in its very *modus operandi* a self-conscious quotation of previous performances – ranging from Welsh praise poetry to the Song of Solomon. Conran is himself rightly fond of bringing an anthropologist's eye to bear on traditional Welsh practices, linking praise poetry, for instance, to the boast poetry of the Bahima of Ankole in Uganda.[13] "Girl Pregnant" is, therefore, the result of reading Welsh praise poetry in the light of analogous practices in other cultures - including the love-poetry and religious poetry of the English Metaphysicals. Conran has used this comparison to bring out the element of high-spirited outrageousness in the way conceits are used in the Welsh tradition. In discussing Dafydd Nanmor's poem "Praise of Rhys ap Maredudd", for instance, he draws particular attention to "the 'play', the fantasy, the serious wit, carried always through the imagery and the closely woven rhythms".[14]

Such wit is present in "Girl Pregnant" not only through the mythopoeic conceits but also in the very ambiguity of the title, which is then amplified in the poem by means of what Conran, in his discussion of the Welsh *cywyddwyr*, called a structural pattern of "counterpoint" (*WV*, 57). "Girl Pregnant" is a descriptive phrase different in implication from "Pregnant Girl", since the latter roughly translates as "girl who is pregnant", whereas the former signifies "girl being pregnant", thus implying that the girl both is and is not to be identified with her pregnancy. The poem is mainly concerned with dramatising the girl's helplessness before the "alien" life force that is transforming her. But then in the last stanza there is a reversal of perspective: "She crowds into a destiny/ That is not hers, though the bow of her/ Slices the covering wave towards her child." Here what was reluctant acquiescence before the inexorable changes into an eagerly incisive act of motherly volition - and these two aspects of her condition are beautifully captured in the pun on "bow". Originally the swollen curve of her belly was seen as her body's response to the pull of alien gravity; but now that curve is re-viewed as the bow of the girl's body-ship headed towards birth and towards fulfilment in accomplished motherhood.

In his discussion of Dafydd Nanmor, Conran mocks Welsh scholars' genteel aversion to finding vulgarly jarring puns in classical Welsh poetry: "Scholars will probably throw their hands up in despair; but this kind of thing happens in other poetry, so why not in Welsh?" (*WV*, 56) There is perhaps more to this remark than meets the eye. Conran is a seriously playful poet. He thrives on the mixed, the impure, the hybrid, revelling in yoking heterogeneous elements together, even if he has to have recourse to a kind of creative violence. This, too, is an aspect of his operating in that space "between foreignness and familiarity." Isn't there a kind of audacious wit involved in his every attempt to "English" peculiarly Welsh forms of poetry or to "Welshify" English poetic usage? One of the most delightfully witty examples in his work of successful cultural cross-fertilisation is "Thirteen Ways of Looking at a Hoover" (*B*8), which consists of thirteen ingenious "descriptions" of a Hoover that between them convey a cubist sense of regarding an object from several different perspectives simultaneously:

iv
The difficult slow ease of scything hay –
It is comparable
To her adroitness with its wheels and flex.

x
Its noise is more sensitive than you'd imagine.
It marks the difference between dusts.

This superb piece can therefore be read either as Wallace Stevens interpreted in the light of the classic Welsh poetic practice of *dyfalu* (i.e. a riddling definition of a person or an object by stringing together a sequence of outrageous tropes), or as *dyfalu* refracted through the poetry of Wallace Stevens ("Thirteen ways of looking at a blackbird"). In other words, it can be understood either as a translation of Welsh into American, or of American into Welsh. And the whole point of the poem (as any one of the great *cywyddwyr* would surely have recognised) is that it is an inter-cultural *tour de force* both of craft and of fantastication.

*   *   *

The emphasis in the foregoing has been on ways in which Tony Conran's encounters, as translator, with Welsh-language literature have significantly altered his relationship, as poet, to the English language and its poetry. As Wolfgang Iser has noted, "reflecting oneself in the other entails heightened self-awareness, which leads to self-confrontation" (*WI*, 32). After a fashion, Conran's poetry involves making English-language poetry a stranger to its customary self – a creative strategy of linguistic self-estrangement that may, of course, be seen as not untypical either of modernist literature or of that important species of so-called post-modernist writing that is closely associated with post-colonial experience. It would, indeed, be possible to argue a case for regarding aspects of Conran's poetry as consciously post-colonial, since one of its aims is to expose the fact that the English-language, as used in classic English literature, is not culturally neutral but heavily complicit in the work of 'anglicisation', that is in conserving and advancing the ideology of Englishness. He also deliberately resists the homogenizing influence of 'inter-national' forms of English, mistrusting it as, in "A Milk Toast", he mistrusts sterilized milk: "sterilized/ Friesan stuff,/ A lingua franca of dairies,/ Minimal enough!" (*B*, 29) His own poetry is dedicated to the subverting of insipidly international English as the *lingua franca* of the modern world: instead, it promotes the idea of many different versions of English, each inflected according to the culture it serves.

As has already been suggested, in his mature work Conran's indebtedness to the Welsh is not always clearly signalled or fore-grounded. It may simply register initially as a powerful "pecu-liarity" of style or an arresting oddity of genre. Yet at least some of his best poetry has continued to depend on the creation of a singular kind of English verse that is specifically advertised as being closely modelled on Welsh strict-metre poetry. His experi-mentations in this manner date right back to his first discovery of Welsh poetry, and constitute attempts to 'translate' not poems but little less than a whole poetics. One of the earliest examples is his imitation of the syllabic pattern (but not the *cynghanedd* or rhyme-scheme) of the staple Welsh *englyn* form, the *englyn unodl union*, in "For the Marriage of Heulwen Evans":

> For you, I invoke old names - Taliesin,
> > With light in his forelocks,
> > That changed before the Huntress
> > To very weft of the wind;

> Gwydion, diviner and poet - who gave
> > A girl's lilt to a rose;
> > For all who'd celebrate love
> > To your love shall be summoned. (*FP*, 5)

This conforms to the requirement that in an *englyn* there must be four lines of ten, six, seven and seven syllables, with the first line being subdivided into a seven-syllable unit before the break (dash/*gwant*) followed by a three-syllable unit (*gair cyrch*) to complete the line. And although no attempt is made here to reproduce the *englyn* rhyme-scheme that would require each 'stanza' to end with a couplet, Conran does at least keep to the rule that of these two lines one must end on a stressed syllable ("wind", "love") and the other on an unstressed syllable ("Huntress", "summoned"). But the overall effect of all this effort is anticlimactic: a case perhaps of old wine in new bottles. The problem is that although Conran has indeed made an attempt (of however rudimentary a kind, judged by his later standards) to emulate the *englyn* form, the actual content of the expression is more Celtic Twilight than Welsh. Before the poem ends there is mention of "the sea dusted with dawn", of "love ... gentle as a moth - stroking/ The moon upon rushes", and of "the calm lake of your Welsh truth". Even allowing for the fact that the rhetoric governing the poem cunningly turns on the claim that this poetry is mere "tatters" compared to the "traditional, intricate praises" of genuine Welsh *barddas*, and that it concludes with the wish that Heulwen Evans' children may "ma[ke] whole/ All fragmentary generations" (such as Conran's own, capable at best of producing only an imperfect, incomplete *englyn*), the impression left by the poetry is of a form of writing being skeletally adopted without any real understanding being manifested of the experiential life of that form in its authentic cultural context. It is almost as if Conran had unconsciously effected a reverse translation - as if in attempting to "translate" an *englyn* into English he had instead turned the *englyn* into a vehicle for expressing an essentially unmodified English sensibility.

Conran also experimented very early on with another staple form of strict-metre poetry, the *cywydd* metre. Again, he sensibly ignored the challenge of *cynghanedd*, and as with the *englyn* his efforts to reproduce only the syllabic measure and distinctive rhythmic profile of the verse met with patchy success. Knowing that Dafydd ap Gwilym has traditionally been credited with introducing the *cywydd* into *cynghanedd* poetry, Conran resourcefully turned to this form when imagining how Dafydd might press his courtship of a young maiden:

> Here, they say, are new-fangled
> Metres, new trash ousting old.
> They cast doubts upon my talent,
> Even as they say, that poor fool!
> He thinks, by taking a common
> Minstrel rhyme, to revive Welsh.
> He thinks too much on women
> (And in particular one girl,
> Her long hair falling, a shimmer
> Of red gold from the broom tree). (*FP*, 16)

93

Years later, Conran was to observe that "the cywydd imposes itself on the phraseology and the syntax of language. It is almost as easily recognizable in translation as Hebrew parallelism."[15] Even in this early example one can see what he means. Nevertheless, this passage is almost as reminiscent of Browning as it is of Dafydd ap Gwilym, and there is about it a slightly bookish air of pastiche.

But these early experimentations, however flawed and unsatisfactory, were to pay rich dividends in due course. As T.S. Eliot (whose work as poet and critic has strongly influenced Conran) once usefully remarked, by "conscious and continuous effort in technical excellence" a poet "is continually developing his medium for the moment when he really has something to say" (*EP*, 17). Conran's elegy for one of the greatest scholars of classic strict-metre poetry, Sir Ifor Williams, is itself one of the classic texts of English-language poetry in modern Wales. It is also a virtuoso technical performance, since it consists of a series of English *englynion* that conform in every particular (including *cynghanedd*) to the demanding rules governing the original Welsh:

> At a loss is Taliesin - the Black Book
> Is bleak, and Aneirin;
> On a bed where learning's been
> The ravens take their ravin.
>
> Sea-eagles feed at midday;
> Too soon they peck at sinew;
> Kite, crow and hawk make outcry;
> Claws upon red flesh they cloy. (*SP*, 97)

The first of these is an *englyn unodl union*, some of the features of which have already been identified above. What additionally needs to be appreciated is that the unit (*gair cyrch*) following the dash in line one should be considered in effect as part of line two. Once it is thus treated, it will be seen that in fact all four lines rhyme ("Taliesin", "Aneirin", "been", "ravin"). Furthermore, each is a line of *canu caeth* (strict metre poetry), and is thus divided into two parts, with the consonants of the second half mirroring those of the first to produce one or other kind of *cynghanedd*, as follows: "At a loss / is Taliesin" (*draws anghytbwys ddisgynedig*); "the Black Book/ is bleak" a mere approximation to *cynghanedd draws*; "On a bed/ where learning's been" (*draws gytbwys acennog - 'n' wreiddgol*); "The ravens/ take their ravin" (*draws gytbwys ddiacen*).[16]

The second 'stanza' is an *englyn lleddfbroest*, a variant of the *englyn proest* whose features have been well summarised by Conran in *Welsh Verse*: "Four lines of seven syllables each, using a peculiar kind of rhyming (called *proest*) in which the final vowels must differ (though not in quantity) while the final consonant remains the same: for example *den, ton, fin* and *ran* form *proest*-rhyme in English."

In the "Elegy for Sir Ifor Williams" Conran succeeds in communicating a strong sense of the "otherness" of the poetry of the Welsh heroic age to the study of which the scholar had devoted so much of his life. And he does so by constructing what Michael Alexander, commenting on Pound's famous version of the great Anglo-Saxon poem "The Seafarer", called a kind of "phonetic simulacrum".[17] Just as Pound, T.S. Eliot acutely noted, "is often most 'original' in the right sense, when he is most 'archaeological' in the ordinary sense" (*EP*, 11), so Conran shows here an extraordinary ability to produce a new mode of writing in English by faithfully re-producing not merely the phonemic patterning but the very grammar and syntax of experience found in the *canu caeth* when it functions as vehicle for a praise tradition, of which elegy is, of course, an important part.

"Throughout the work of Pound", wrote Eliot, "there is what might be called a steady effort towards the synthetic construction of a style of speech. In each of the elements or strands there is something of Pound and something of some other, not further analysable" (*EP*, 12). Pound's work as translator, he added, contributed substantially to the development of Pound as a poet, since "good translation...is not merely translation, for the translator is giving the original through himself, and finding himself through the original." These observations apply almost equally well to the work and poetic career of Tony Conran. As he matured in his craft as translator, so did he take unto and into himself as poet not just the intricate technicalities of the *canu caeth* but the modes of sensibility of a whole "other" culture.

Poetry in performance: Tony and Lesley Conran

According to Raymond Williams' useful formulation, structures of form are also structures of feeling. Conran has made his own way to such an insight, not by slowly assimilating Welsh poetry in some mystically organicist fashion, but by methodically analysing the deep structure of its foreign forms so that he is able, when he wishes, to engineer in English a feeling of cultural "otherness" without imitating Welsh forms as minutely as he did in the "Elegy for Sir Ifor Williams". After all, that was appropriately and necessarily an "occasional" poem: to have repeated such a feat would have been to condemn himself to a kind of ultimately crippling literalness of the imagination.

★　　★　　★

Conran's greatest success in this "freer" mode, and in "the synthetic construction of a style of speech" is probably his elegy (or synthetic *awdl*) for the Welsh soldiers who died at Bluff Cove during the Falklands/Malvinas War:

> Men went to Catraeth. The luxury liner
> For three weeks feasted them.
> They remembered easy ovations,
> Our boys, splendid in courage.
> For three weeks the albatross roads,
> Passwords of dolphin and petrel,
> Practised their obedience
> Where the killer whales gathered,
> Where the monotonous seas yelped.
> Though they went to church with their standards
> Raw death has them garnished. (*B*, 14)

In this opening passage, and throughout the poem, Conran's seriously playful wit is much in evidence. The first line deliberately isolates an absurd anachronism for our puzzled attention ("Men went to Catraeth. The luxury liner"), and by the second line the clash of archaic and modern registers of speech has already been jarringly established ("The luxury liner/... feasted them"). As the ritualistic pattern of the verse itself suggests ("For three weeks ... For three weeks"; "Passwords ... Practised"; "Where the ... Where the"), this is to be a poem about parallelisms (between present and past) that are both symmetric and asymmetric, comforting and disquieting, heroic and ironic. It is out of the interplay between such fearful symmetries that the tragic vision of the poem is to emerge.

Of late, Conran has increasingly insisted on describing himself as a writer of tragedy, and has expressed an intense interest in older forms of tragedy, where the plight of an individual focusses the plight of a whole society.[18] "Elegy for the Welsh Dead in the Falkland Islands, 1982" is itself tragedy in that mode, the tragedy of a Wales that is lost in history because it has lost sight of its own history, the "otherness" of which is felt to haunt this poem by virtue of the felt foreignness of both the ancient references and the strange 'body language' of the verse. That history, of which the young soldiers are as unaware as they are of Aneirin's *Gododdin* (the sixth century poem in which "Men went to Catraeth" to be slaughtered), is the hidden cruelty of fate that is so destructively at work in and upon their lives:

> With the dawn men went. Those forty-three,
> Gentlemen all, from the streets and byways of Wales,
> Dragons of Aberdare, Denbigh and Neath –
> Figment of empire, whore's honour, held them.
> Forty-three at Catraeth died for our dregs.

The Welsh are appropriately among the last to fall victim to that vision of British Empire to which they have so eagerly subscribed ever since Tudor times, suppressing in the process all memory of their own separate history, that stretches back to the period of the *Gododdin*. As Conran has noted, "Tragedy is about now, but its method of dealing with it is metaphorical. The tragic world, like a miracle play, is fundamentally anachronistic. It may claim to be about the remote past, but actually, like a symphony, like a great ballet, it lives in its own time, tangential to all our worlds" (*BM*, 15) His unremittingly dark elegy brings Aneirin's ancient poem tangentially to bear on the Welsh present, to powerfully tragic effect. The young soldiers (addressed as "Gentlemen all", in a quintessentially English turn of phrase used here with a combination of irony and sincerity) are represented as the victims not only of Margaret Thatcher's aggressive chauvinism but also of a Welsh "nation" culpably besotted with a Britishness that has left it economically devastated ("Aberdare, Denbigh and Neath"), fertile ground only for military recruitment.

A similar vision of Wales and its history informs Conran's fine recent sequence *Castles*, a complex composite that is at once personal and public, historical and mythic, political and psychological. Contributing to its rich texture is an elegy for Linda Noyau into which Conran poignantly weaves the poem he had originally written for her wedding decades earlier:

> *On the spry thyme, saffron-heeled Hymen*
> *would once (in weaving torchlit dances*
> *appropriate to a great god's greeting)*
> *have given these leave to live as lovers -*
> > *they who marry this blithe morrow, and now*
> > *their doom doubt, prow out over wild waters.*

You re-make poems every time they're read -
Nothing strange in that. Marriage and funeral

> Are metaphors, one of another. And for Linda
> In whom light was alive, it would not demean
> Her death, dressing her in the white brocade of a
>   wedding ..[19]

As Conran goes on to recall, the prothalamion was "Arnaut's *sestina* under-read/ With *cynghanedd* plucked for their wedding/ From Dafydd Nanmor's *gwawdodyn*." And as he now re-reads that poem, its metaphors begin to resonate with different implications, born of new contexts of meaning: "metaphors in the poem/ Make their circumference the occasions where it's read". It is a significant moment, not least because it makes explicit what is usually left implicit, namely the way a poet continues to develop by re-reading himself, as it were; that is, he grows by reinterpreting, and re-wording, his central preoccupations in the light of changing circumstances. Moreover, there is a sense in which his "recycling" of his prothalamion offers a paradigm for understanding the way in which Conran's interest in Welsh-language poetry has served him well as a poet in his own right. As he says, "You re-make poems every time they're read". His reading of Welsh-language poetry has indeed involved a complex and still ongoing process of re-making, in which the past, as inscribed in Welsh-language texts, and the present, that Conran of course seeks to address in his own poetry, have come to function (in part through the very otherness of their inalienable difference) as "metaphors, one of another."

Conran has always emphasised that to translate is very hard work:

> So hard – the hazard is huge
> I deal against a deluge
> While a dotty world yet wags
> Trumps from a thousand handbags! (*SP*, 96)

In this English *cywydd* about the near-impossibility of writing an English *cywydd* Conran goes on to characterise his efforts as "Heart's clamour, labour of lathe." These are also the skills and energies (of intensely committed heart and cool head) he has needed in order to be able to translate translation into original poetry. This brings to mind Eliot's wise words about the work of his old friend Ezra Pound:

> To consider Pound's original work and his translation separately would be a mistake, a mistake which implies a greater mistake about the nature of translation ... If Pound had not been a translator his reputation as an 'original' poet would be higher; if he had not been an original poet, his reputation as a 'translator' would be higher; and this is all irrelevant. (*EP*,15)

Like Pound (and indeed like many contemporary writers, such as Tony Harrison, W.S. Merwin, and Thomas Kinsella), Tony Conran is a fine poet because he is a fine translator, and is likewise a fine translator because he is a fine poet. Any further attempts to explain his impressive case would be "all irrelevant." After all, both poetry and translation are naturally complementary modes of creative expression for one who is, above everything and in everything he does, a "shaman of shifting form".

Notes

1.Anthony Conran, autobiographical essay, in Meic Stephens, ed., *Artists in Wales: 2* (Llandysul: Gwasg Gomer, 1973), 111-123.

2. "Anglo-Welsh manqué: on the selected poems of Bobi Jones", *Planet* 76 (1989), 68. Hereafter *BJ*. I am very grateful to my friend Dr Tony Brown, University of Wales, Bangor, for providing me with an advance copy of his "Tony Conran: a bibliography".

3. "The Uncommitted Persona: a review of *Selected Poems* by Leslie Norris", *Planet* 62 (1987), 94.

4. T.S.Eliot, "Introduction" (1928) to the *Selected Poems of Ezra Pound* (London: Faber, 1969 edition), 11. Hereafter *EP*.

5. Tony Conran, "An invocation of Angels" in *Formal Poems* (Denbigh: Gwasg Gee, 1960), 24. Hereafter *FP*.

6. "The Blade", *Spirit Level* (Llandybie: Christopher Davies, 1974), 15. Hereafter *SL*.

7. "Elegy for Brenda Chamberlain", *Life Fund* (Llandysul: Gwasg Gomer, 1979), 51, Hereafter *LF*.

8. "My poem pictures the scientist's desire to know as a kind of greed in which the ego wants to swallow the whole world". (Note on "Space", *SL*, 136.)

9. Wolfgang Iser, "On Translatability: Variables of Interpretation", in *The European English Messenger* IV/l (Spring, 1995), 30, 32, 33. Hereafter *WI*.

10. "Tony Conran Interview", in *Materion Dwyieithog/Bilingual Matters* 3 (1991), 11-12. Hereafter *BM*.

11. "Blodeuwedd", in *Blodeuwedd and other poems* (Bridgend: Poetry Wales Press, 1988), 60. Hereafter *B*.

12. "Gerard Hopkins as an Anglo-Welsh poet", in William Tydeman, ed., *The Welsh Connection* (Llandysul: Gwasg Gomer, 1986), 118.

13. "Tribal poetry and the Gogynfeirdd", *Planet* 99 (1993), 47-58. See also his poem "Ebyevugo", *LF*, 67-69.

14. Tony Conran, Introduction to *Welsh Verse* (Bridgend: Poetry Wales Press, 1986), 55. Hereafter *WV*.

15. Review article on Rachel Bromwich, *Dafydd ap Gwilym: a selection of poems*, *The Anglo-Welsh Review* 75 (1984), 85.

16. I am grateful to Dr Peredur Lynch, and to my daughter, Elin, for assistance in this analysis.

17. Quoted in Peter Brooker, *A Student's Guide to the Selected Poems of Ezra Pound* London: Faber (1979), 72.

18. "The Debatable Land: Tony Conran on the tension in his work between lyric and tragedy", *Planet* 90 (1991-92), 55-65; also the interview in *Materion Dwyieithog/Bilingual Matters*, 15-16.

19. Section IV, Variation xxiv ("Sestina on sestina"), of *Castles* (Llandysul: Gwasg Gomer, 1993), 53-55.

Constructing a Critical Space
Ned Thomas

Anglo-Welsh poetry differs from other poetry in the English language in three main respects. First, it has in its background, a different civilization - it is like English poetry written by Irishmen or Indians. Second, it shares its territory with another linguistic community which regards its tongue as the right and natural language of the country - a claim which Anglo-Welsh writers often accept, and which even if they dispute, they cannot ignore. In this respect, Anglo-Welsh poetry is like English poetry written by Nigerians or Maoris. Thirdly, it derives from a special sort of society, which I shall call 'the buchedd' from a Welsh word meaning 'a way of life' or 'ethos'. In this third aspect, it is more like poetry in English written by Americans. American society, like Welsh, was consciously without an upper-class, deliberately egulitarian, puritanical in morals, a product of cultural revolution following the break-up of accepted social patterns.[1]

I start with this text not in order to lead us into the marshes of definition, nor to claim that this is a comprehensive statement of Tony Conran's position, but for the light it throws on the critic's own practice, the way he sets about constructing a space of its own for Anglo-Welsh poetry.

The first thing we need to note is that Conran, though showing in passing a wide knowledge of Anglo-Welsh prose, is, as a critic, almost entirely concerned with *poetry*. He is, of course, himself a poet and a translator of poetry, which makes him a close reader of the poetic text, and a hearer of the text. He has a strong pre-occupation with form, whether he is expounding intricate systems such as Welsh *cynghanedd* and the self-conscious metrics of Gerard Manley Hopkins, or seeking an underlying structure for Idris Davies's *The Angry Summer*. But beyond all this, what energizes his criticism is that he is committed to the idea that poetic form has *social* significance.

Yet if poetic form is socially significant, surely other literary forms will have their own social meaning, and a shift between literary forms may also be indicative of a social shift. Of another critic one might be content to say that the overwhelming concern with poetry was merely the expression of a personal preference. Because of Conran's concern with the social significance of form, the relegation of prose to the margins of his criticism deserves some attention. How does a critic who is so patently interested in the social and class configurations of Wales in the twentieth century come to show so little critical interest in the Anglo-Welsh novels and short stories that at one time seemed almost the dominant mode?

One part of the answer must be that in poetry, and in the social role of the poet, he finds it possible to argue a continuity between Welsh and Anglo-Welsh literature in a way that it would be hard to do for the novel where the connections between Anglo-Welsh and English are more apparent. In other words, the emphasis on poetry is part of the construction of a *different* space for the Anglo-Welsh writer to inhabit - different, that is, from the English writer. It is worth taking this question a little further.

Of his own work Conran wrote:

I have never been interested in writing prose fiction.

> For one thing I could never think of plots; and for
> another, the precise notation of experience - even
> imaginary experience - on its own terms - has never
> meant much to me as a creative artist.[2]

Now "the precise notation of experience" also goes on in poetry,
indeed it characterises a great deal of modern and contemporary
poetry in English; but this is a kind of poetry that Conran per-
ceives as not in the Welsh tradition. The communal, the celebratory - *these* are the backbone of the Welsh tradition for Conran,
whether they are found in mediaeval Welsh poetry or in Idris
Davies.

> It was very hard work for a Welshman, even a
> monoglot English-speaking Welshman, to write like an
> English poet. There was, as we say, no traditional bias
> towards empiricism in the culture he came from.
> Poems in Welsh were made for a practical purpose, to
> praise a lord, or God, or to amuse, or edify, or to com-
> pete for a prize. They are rarely just records of experi-
> ence, data presented or knowledge gained.[3]

That last sentence recalls the phrase "the precise notation of
experience" quoted earlier. But we see now that it is not just
prose fiction that lies outside the tradition Conran is invoking.
His commitment is to a particular kind of poetry, and Anglo-
Welsh poets can be placed on a scale that measures their distance
from that tradition:

> There is a continuous spectrum nowadays between
> Anglo-Welsh poets like Idris Davies and Dylan
> Thomas who write almost totally non-empiricist verse
> (Dylan's prose is a slightly different matter) and those

like Jean Earle or John Davies who mostly seem indis-
tinguishable from English poets in the way they com-
pose.[4]

Normally Conran's preferences exist within a sense of the complexity and variety of individual situations that is highly tolerant.
But just occasionally we are made aware that he considers the
wrong choice to be a kind of betrayal. This is the case in his discussion of Leslie Norris's version of Gwenallt's poem "Y
Meirwon":

> It is an extraordinary emasculation of a poem, and
> one is entitled to ask why Norris chose to "imitate"
> (to use Lowell's word) Gwenallt's elegy in this
> destructively namby-pamby way. That it is deliberate
> is certain: no-one mistranslates "lilies pale as gas" as
> "lilies pale as ice" without knowing what they're
> doing. The change from "silicotic roses" to "gasping
> roses" is instructive: "gasping" may certainly be one
> connotation of "silicotic", but it lays all the stress on
> the physical sufferings of the roses themselves.
> "Silicotic" - which I take as basically a synonym for
> blood-red referring back to the red mess in the bucket
> earlier in the poem - is not primarily descriptive of the
> roses but of the sufferings to which they pay tribute
> ....
> At any rate, Norris made a full-blooded attempt to
> translate "Y Meirwon" into his own idiom and mode,
> even at the cost of scrapping much of the imagery
> and particularity of the original. We can see what he
> has to leave out of the reckoning, and that the remain-
> der is almost a paradigm of what his poetry in general
> has to ignore in order to exist; that is, it tabulates the

cost of fashioning for himself an uncommitted "voice" in the English manner. The detachment of exile or "Britishness" is one option for the Anglo-Welsh writer; but, to chose it means a self-wounding limitation on the power to see life clearly and to see it whole.[5]

The opening sentence of the text quoted at the start of this essay revealed two basic and related assumptions: that poetry is the central area of concern, and that within this area Conran wants to establish what differentiates Wales from England. The discussion of the Norris translation shows that this is not a merely academic enquiry but a passionate personal commitment to social and maybe political aims.

*   *   *

An important part of Conran's critical work has been the interpretation of the poetry of what in our opening text he calls "a different civilization" - that is, the poetry of Celtic and mediaeval Wales which he so successfully and extensively translated in the *Penguin Book of Welsh Verse* (the original volume stopped in 1600). I am not qualified to assess his scholarship in this field, and my concern here, in any case, is to relate this work to other aspects of his criticism; but I think a specialist's view might be that while he does not always show familiarity with the latest details of academic investigation in this field, this is compensated for by approaches and comparisons that are fresh, adventurous and illuminating.

It is important to Tony Conran to stress the 'difference' of this early civilization not in a simply historical sense but in a 'national' sense. Although he admits that the high civilization of Wales has become for the Welsh people today "no more than a vague memory, becoming more than that only in certain metrical habits unique to the country, and possibly in a respect for poets and poetry not otherwise accounted for"[6] this understates, as we have seen, the importance he attaches to the Welsh poetic tradition. Moreover "the exploration of the lost civilization by scholars and writers was one way in which the aspiration of a new middle class expressed and defined itself in both Welsh and English."[7] Presumably it is within that pattern of exploration that Conran's own translation and interpretative work is to be placed. That it has this dynamic purpose is confirmed by the Penguin volume which he offered "To the People of Wales".

However, he perhaps too easily assumes that what is going on in Welsh and English is the same thing. The "exploration of the lost civilization" within the Welsh language is not the same experience psychologically as the exploration starting from English. For the first group, it is not an experience of simple difference but of strange familiarity, an enlargement of the world transmitted by the language, a broadening of the set of terms within which life in Welsh is lived. Saunders Lewis delighted in emphasizing - and maybe over-emphasizing - the continental connections and dimensions of Welsh literature which study of the Welsh Middle Ages can reveal; the Welshness of that literature can be taken for granted because of the language. Tony Conran's exploration is better called discovery. A difference of language and a difference of culture is encountered at the same time. Like every discovery, it is selective. The elements which Conran finds are those which he values and identifies with (which we have already touched on) and which serve to distinguish Wales from England. It is that same quality of excited selective discovery that makes for a good translator of poetry, since translation is necessarily a kind of selective reading.

★　　★　　★

The next way in which Conran makes Anglo-Welsh poetry distinctive is by relating it to what, in the passage quoted at the head
of this essay, he calls the buchedd, a special sort of society with
an egalitarian, Nonconformist culture, that was dominant at least
up to the First World War, and that lasted long enough for
Conran himself to have encountered it in person in north Wales,
and for his well-tuned ear to hear its echoes in the English of
Huw Menai, Idris Davies and T. Harri Jones, the subjects of
some of his best critical essays.(I don't italicize 'buchedd'
because Conran has made its meaning in English his own, self-
confessedly adapting to his purpose a word that has a range of
meanings in Welsh, none quite the Conran meaning).

It is part of Conran's case that this culture was broader than
language, and held together both Welsh-speaking and non-
Welsh-speaking Welsh people. In general terms that is true,
though it is clear from Conran's treatment of Anglo-Welsh poets
that with education and social mobility the slippage in language
helped open up a cultural tension because it let in an English,
middle-class culture. This is evident in varying degrees in: Huw
Menai (scarcely at all), in Idris Davies increasingly (what
Conran terms his *embourgeoisement*) and in Alun Lewis to the
point of making like impossible. In each of these cases, the connection with Welsh and with the buchedd, the slippage to
English, and the tension that opens up can be plotted in terms of
the individual life and the family background. But Conran's
argument goes beyond this.

He uses W.H. Davies (who had no Welsh in his background and
came from Newport) to develop a wider notion of cultural influence across the division of language, the notion of "seepage"
which is utterly crucial to Conran's critical project. W.H. Davies's
ideas of what constituted a poet and poetry, it is argued, were
influenced by assumptions from the Welsh tradition of folk-poet-
ry, itself the social creation of the Welsh people. "What I have

109

called seepage", writes Conran, "is one of the reasons why Anglo-Welsh poetry belongs to us, the people of Wales, and is not to be hived off as interesting but minor English verse."[8] Difference from England is again asserted, this time at the level of popular poetry and popular life.

There are some parallels to be drawn here with the work of reclamation which Peter Lord has been carrying out on Welsh country painters, the *arlunwyr gwlad,* and also with what Margaret Atwood found herself doing in *Survival* where she sought to uncover and define the separate nature of Canadian literature in English. In each case there is a sense of needing to re-evaluate not the high achievers by metropolitan standards, but what has been regarded as the artistic undergrowth. Although Conran has some very astute points to make on certain aspects of Dylan Thomas or R.S. Thomas, I have never felt that he excels when he addresses them in their entirety; while his re-evaluation of the 'lesser' writers changes the whole climate of opinion.

Conran's emphasis on what he calls the buchedd is all the more valuable because it eschews two competing and influential rhetorics. On the one hand, literary culture in Welsh since Saunders Lewis, though partly tied to the institutions of chapel and Eisteddfod, has been distancing itself from traditional Nonconformity and from the amateur culture that went with it. Language nationalism has an uneasy relationship with and finds it difficult to do justice to the period which was the heyday of Conran's buchedd when a strongly Welsh-speaking working-class (industrial as well as rural) generally embraced a British ideology. But on the other hand, a great deal of Anglo-Welsh writing has defined itself as escaping from Nonconformist culture, and either treated it with scorn or averted its eyes.

Conran, standing outside these tensions, shows a comprehensive understanding of the popular strengths of the culture, and of the social landslide that carried it away.

Idris Davies's poetry is poised, it seems to me, on the breakdown of the buchedd-culture of the South. His greatest work incarnates and mourns buchedd values, far more than it does socialism or simply working-class bitterness or hope. As the hymns of Pantycelyn were the poetry of its inception, so the elegies of *Gwalia Deserta* and the quasi-drama of *The Angry Summer* are the real expression of the buchedd's collapse.[9]

That reading of Idris Davies makes some very broad sweeps and perhaps underestimates other perspectives that can illuminate his work; but it makes greater and more cohesive sense of the variety of tones in Idris Davies, and of the particularity of the place and time than does a simple proletarian reading. Moreover Conran understands very clearly that a reaction against Nonconformist culture is never a total escape:

Anglo-Welsh poetry, quite as much as Anglo-Welsh fiction, was a product of the buchedd-society, its defeat and break-up. Even a modernist like the young Dylan Thomas wrote his poetry against that background, consciously in rebellion against buchedd-values.[10]

Once again, in the discussion that he opens up around his notion of buchedd, we see that Conran has managed to establish a distinctive space in which the literature of Wales in English can be understood in one period.

★   ★   ★

Conran's second defining criterion for Anglo-Welsh poetry - "it shares its territory with another linguistic community" - I take third. It is the most problematic in Conran's criticism, but not for the reasons we are most used to. He neither romanticizes nor is hostile to Welsh-language culture, and, as we have seen, his account of Anglo-Welsh poetry makes it both continuous and discontinuous with the Welsh tradition. The whole essay "Pilgrims from a Desert Land" is a magnificently complex account of the limitations and potential of the two languages at a particular historical moment. I can't do more here than give a sense of the quality of the argument:

> Losing one language and acquiring another is a complicated process. Welsh critics have naturally tended to see it as largely one of cultural loss. The result, they say, is neither English nor Welsh, but a kind of limbo creature of the wasteland. There's a lot of truth in what they say. The process is accompanied by a lot of silly snobbery. There's often a sense of cultural deprivation, a truculence that betrays an inferiority complex; even a wholesale failure to articulate more than bread-and-butter meanings. Patterns of thought which in the parent speech would have been integrated into a whole way of life are left loose and noisy on the surface of the mind. People become linguistic opportunists, at the mercy of short-term emotions. Style becomes either a conformity to standards borrowed from elsewhere and only partially assimilated; or a series of 'existentialist' gestures, what is 'hip' and 'flashy'.
>
> ....
>
> That's not the whole story, though. If the linguistic change accompanies a mighty convulsion in the fabric

of society or a great widening in social opportunity, as
it did among immigrants to the United States or in the
coal-mining valleys of South Wales, the parent languages - Welsh or Lithuanian or Yiddish - may not be
able to confront the situation at all adequately. Some
sort of atavistic response, seeing the new world only in
terms of what is lost, may be a temptation written into
the language you use. Most of the time indeed, the old
culture may just forget the new situation exists at all
.... The obsessions are elsewhere. And because the
obsessions are elsewhere, and because the basic element of the situation *is* an exploding fragmentation of
what it has meant to be human, the new language may
in fact be stronger, more culturally apposite than the
old.[11]

Conran then goes on to compare Gwenallt's "Y Meirwon" with
Idris Davies's *The Angry Summer* 4, sensitive to the immediately
perceivable strengths of the former but breaking new ground to
reveal a strong sense of the future in the Idris Davies.

Let me quote the final stanza of the Idris Davies and a little of
Conran's commentary, which starts with detailed, textual appreciation and ends with broad cultural sweeps.

> Shine softly, moon, upon their sleep,
> And, poet, in your music keep
> Their memory alive and fair,
> Echoing in the electric air.

Nor is the music of the piece to be despised, the way it
shimmers as the iambics break down at the end into
flickering short syllables, vowel eliding into vowel ....
Many people have felt this tenderness towards the

113

dead, but it is certainly not a cliché. Above all, there is
the sense we have in any poem of Idris Davies (at least
before his final phase of disillusionment, and even
there in some fashion) that the poetry is open-ended,
refuses to draw a line under life and call it finished,
even if the good is defeated and the beautiful ravaged
by greed.

It is for these sorts of reason that we have to balance
Gwenallt's "Y Meirwon" not just with any single lyric
of Idris Davies's but with one or other of the
sequences, with the whole mosaic, *Gwalia Deserta* or
The Angry Summer, for anything less botches his form.
And in that sort of balance, with the teeming sense of
life, the good humour, the hope, the very healthy kind
of anger, the compassion that does not lose its bearings in the sufferings of others, with all that on one
side of the equation, it is not at all obvious that the
Gwenallt - for all its power - is the greater poem of the
two. On the contrary, it is Idris Davies who emerges as
what we always knew he was, the poet of the Valleys,
that unique society in its travail and dereliction.[12]

This is a necessary balancing case that is put and put excellently.
And because Conran's sensitivity is so rooted in an understanding of a particular historical moment, we are not using dead
poets for the purposes of contemporary polemic. After all, we
live with a wholly different set of social forces now.

If I nevertheless see the relation of Anglo-Welsh to Welsh, and
indeed of Anglo-Welsh to English, as a problematic area in Tony
Conran's criticism, it is for reasons connected with his central
project, the creation of a distinct Anglo-Welsh space. The difficulty I draw attention to is to some extent built into all cross-cultural criticism.

Conran is seeking to locate Anglo-Welsh poetry between Welsh-language literary and social tradition on the one hand, and the English middle-class literary tradition on the other. The problem is not merely that the ideal critic needs an encyclopaedic knowledge of all three elements (and the critic's critic even more so), but that all three elements are changing so that it is extremely difficult to hold the whole process in focus. Conran's main focus is on the situation of the Anglo-Welsh whom he sees in complex and evolving social, political, linguistic and class terms, discontinuous inheritors but also claimants to a new world. By comparison, the Welsh-language world is presented not exactly as unchanging but in terms of its continuities and valued essences (for Conran) and only insofar as its social experience is mirrored however distantly in English-speaking Wales. Conran is unsettled by the prospect that Welsh-speakers might find more experience in common with other linguistic minorities.

The Gwenallt/Idris Davies comparison (above) is a good example of an Anglo-Welsh focus. We are asked to look at the spread of Idris Davies poems, and that reinforces Conran's point. If we looked at the spread of Gwenallt we would soon find that in Conran's phrase "the obsessions are elsewhere". We are dealing with the industrial valley in tension with the culture of rural Wales. But how many points can one make at the same time?

Elsewhere Conran argues that consciousness of sharing its territory with another language became an important feature in Anglo-Welsh poetry

> mostly after 1955 or so when Welsh-speakers became aggressively defensive of their rights. Up to that time Welsh people spoke what language suited them as luck, geography or social pressures dictated; but English and Welsh-speakers belonged to the same community and very largely shared the same range of outlooks.[13]

Whereas the conclusion is one I have already agreed with, what goes before is a merry kind of pastoral. It is never luck that determines what language people speak, though it may sometimes seem so if the question is posed at the individual level; nor is linguistic geography the harmless neutral phenomenon it claims to be - it is linguistic politics and linguistic history in spatial form. "Social pressures" lets the cat out of the bag. The pressures were there and were evident to some people long before 1955 - to Emrys ap Iwan and Michael D. Jones, to T. Gwynn Jones and Saunders Lewis and the founders of the Welsh Nationalist Party. Of course Conran knows all this, but here his eye is fixed on the Anglo-Welsh, who may well have only become aware that there was a 'language-problem' in 1955.

'Seepage', as we have already seen, is an immensely suggestive concept, plausible in general terms, though extremely difficult to pin down in practice outside the family context. I am not entirely convinced by the case of W.H. Davies, partly because I would want to know more about popular levels of poetry in English at the time, including in America where Davies spent many years of his life. Is it really Welsh poetic and popular tradition that informs that part of Davies's work which Conran commends? English poetry tends to be typed in Conran as the official, middle-class tradition, and since this tradition is more dominant in English culture than in Welsh, the typing is up to a point legitimate; but it is not the only tradition in England. This again is something Conran knows well, but where would his argument on 'seepage' be if he looked in that direction all the time? Once more we are brought up against the difficulty of holding different strands in focus at the same time and allowing each of them a life and complexity of its own. One is made more aware of this difficulty in a climate where post-colonial criticism emphasizes internal division and cross-cultural connection rather than the simpler centre/periphery opposition.

There are more immediate and practical problems for Conran's criticism in the 'eighties and 'nineties. Always sensitive to the contemporary political and literary atmosphere, and generous in his approach to individual writers, Conran has more recently had to contend with a literary scene very different from that of the 'sixties and 'seventies which better fitted his preoccupations. He admits, for example, that the work of Dannie Abse had long been at the edges of his Anglo-Welsh gaze, and then goes on to write a very thorough critical essay on his work, though almost entirely outside an Anglo-Welsh frame. In dealing with Tony Curtis, on the other hand, Conran seems to be searching for a new and emergent set of Anglo-Welsh qualities that will encompass that part of Curtis's work that appeals to him. But this is nothing like a worked-out position.

The immediate context of the present literary scene with its 'Wales-based' writers and instant literary events is not favourable to the kind of critical work which is characteristic of Conran - complex, deeply historical and deeply committed. But popular consciousness is more historically retentive than is the arts scene, and the need to know who you are and where you come from persists both at the individual and the group level. In the precarious territory of the Anglo-Welsh (a term which he does not reject) Conran keeps open a space in which readers - who do not have to be literary professionals to understand him - may hear the resonance of their own lives and those of their families and communities.

Notes

In the writing of this essay I have had access to the typescript of a forthcoming volume of essays by Tony Conran, referred to below provisionally as *SAWP* (*Studies in Anglo-Welsh Poetry*), necessarily without page numbers. Some of the individual essays in this collection can also be traced to their original source through the bibliography included in this volume, but the original version may not always be identical with the text revised for *SAWP* which I have used.

1. "The 'Welsh Way of Life' and its Poetry" in *SAWP*.
2. "Fairy Tales" in *Planet* 105 (1994), 87-92.
3. "The Anglo-Welsh Vanishing Point - the Eastaway of Edward Thomas" in *SAWP*.
4. *Ibid.* in *SAWP*.
5. "Telling the Dead Go Home: the Poetry of Leslie Norris" in *SAWP*.
6. "The 'Welsh Way of Life' and its Poetry" in *SAWP*.
7. *Ibid.* in *SAWP*.
8."The Tramp Poems of W.H.Davies" in *The Cost of Strangeness* (Llandysul 1982), 35.
9. "The 'Welsh Way of Life' and its Poetry" in *SAWP*.
10. *Ibid.* in *SAWP*.
11. "Pilgrims from a Desert Land" in *SAWP*.
12. *Ibid.* in *SAWP*.
13. "The 'Welsh Way of Life' and its Poetry" in *SAWP*.

Tony Conran's "Gift" Poems in Context
Ian Gregson

Tony Conran is most accurately seen as a member of a generation of poets which has suffered from the way that the
Movement poetic dominated the British poetry world in the
'fifties and 'sixties. Conran was born in 1931 which means that
his writing career overlaps with that, for example, of Edwin
Morgan (born 1920), Christopher Middleton (born 1926) and
Roy Fisher (born 1930) - as it does also with that of Larkin
(born 1922) and with that of Larkin's poetic opposite John
Ashbery (born 1927). However, where Larkin is most accurately
regarded as anti-modernist, and John Ashbery as postmodernist,
these poets can best be seen as retro-modernist. In inventing this
term I am referring to the extent to which they owe their most
important allegiance to the classic modernism of the 1920s, to
the generation of Eliot, Pound, Williams and Joyce, born about
forty years before them - though they have also built upon the
assumptions of that tradition in their own individual ways.

This makes them profoundly unlike Larkin - most symptomati-
cally in their anti-realism. Unlike his, their poems do not characteristically construct a reliable sense of the poet's self authorita-
tively describing and commenting on self-consciously familiar
slices of life. However, their anti-realism does not involve, as
Ashbery's does, a playful celebration of the impossibility of ever
fully apprehending the real: instead it contains a fraught nostalgia both for epistemological assurance and ontological authenticity. Larkin and Ashbery both make assumptions, though of an

opposite kind; for these retro-modernists, by contrast the nature of the real is always in question and the experimental forms of their writing are evolved in an attempt to grasp it while simultaneously acknowledging its elusiveness.

For this reason, the concept of estrangement, or defamiliarisation, is crucial to these poets, as it is to classic modernism and as it is not for either Larkin - who harps on the familiar - or for Ashbery who harps on the strange, or for whom reality is such an all-embracing problem it ceases to be a problem. For their constant interrogation of the real means that their poems enact continual but creative failures to grasp it which, in the process of that failure, continually defamiliarise it.

It is because they share this preoccupation with the inventor of the concept of "estrangement", Viktor Shlovsky - himself very much a writer of the classic modernist period - that, like him, these poets are so concerned with issues of perception. Their poems repeatedly dwell self-reflexively on mind/object relations, on the status and meaning of their own images, and Shklovsky himself stressed the estranging effect this self-reflexiveness has when he said that

> This new attitude to objects in which, in the last analysis, the object becomes perceptible, is that artificiality which, in our opinion, creates art. A phenomenon, perceived many times, and no longer perceivable, or rather, the method of such dimmed perception, is what I call "recognition" as opposed to "seeing". The aim of imagery, the aim of creating new art is to return the object from "recognition" to "seeing".[1]

For these retro-modernists, as for Shklovsky, this preoccupattion has led to a constant interrogation of images and of the image-centred styles (imagism, expressionism, surrealism) of classic modernism - Conran, as I shall show, evolved his later poetic partly in a sceptical dialogue with imagism. However, what distinguishes him from Morgan, Fisher and Middleton is his engagement with Welsh poetic tradition. So, while the questioning, self-conscious poetic which characterises the early Conran anticipates the sceptical retro-modernism of the later poet, it seems to have been his growth in political understanding which was crucial in transforming the one into the other. This is most explicitly in evidence in *The Cost of Strangeness*,[2] his book on Anglo-Welsh poetry, where he is revealed as an astute analyst of Welsh social history. This book shows how distant the later Conran is from the political inadvertance of "The Swan"[3] - with its nostalgia for a lost Eden of non-arbitrary naming - and "Elegiac Ode for R. Williams Parry" (*Poems*, 31-4) . It shows him, for instance, dismissing the facile nostalgia for an original Wales:

> Others turned to some form of atavistic romanticism ... A purely literary day-dreaming about the long-ago heroic Wales before Edward I was a dangerous antidote to the frustrations of living in the humdrum chapel-going Wales of the present. (167)
>
> ....
>
> The typical Anglo-Welsh poem of the 'sixties ... became an elegy for the Welsh Way of Life, in one or other of its many aspects: an elegy that signs the death warrant of its subject, asserts that it is thoroughly dead, in order that the poet may define his stance, defiant or pathetic, in the act of acknowledging the demise. The elegy both mitigates the guilt of middle-class separation from the tribe, and reinforces that separation. (233)

121

The later Conran has successfully avoided such sterile elegy by choosing two quite distinct models - Welsh praise poetry and European modernism. This has had fascinating results because the former emphasises the social role of the poet and the latter is insistently sceptical and questioning; the result is the creation of a poetic which constantly interrogates both society and poetry.

There is much in modernism that has necessarily not interested Conran, and he has been opposed to some of its aspects. The emphasis in the movement that has been most important to him has been that upon the artificiality of the arts: under the influence of the avant-garde composer Bernard Rands, he was made aware "of the arbitrary nature of pattern. One can, so to speak, choose one's co-ordinates". (*Poems*, "Introduction", xix).

The aspect of modernism to which Conran has been opposed is that which has been most readily domesticated in British poetry - the technical devices of imagism. Some of his poems actually reflect upon imagist inadequacies in order to transcend them; the controlling image in "Space"[4] reflects upon the idea of controlling images. The "grid" referred to is the device once used by painters to help them judge perspective – this involved setting a frame with a network of threads between the artist's eye and his subject, the squares were then drawn on the paper, and a spot was placed on the net to serve as a fixed point. The poem takes this as an obvious example of the way that space is domesticated for us, made safer, by our conventions of seeing:

> URGENCY IS A HOLE KEPT IN PLACE BY BARS.
> OTHERWISE I SHOULD BURST. MY SIDES WOULD COLLAPSE.
> TOO MANY SPACES POUR INTO ONE SWOLLEN EYE.
> VERY WELL, I PARTITION MY EYE INTO TEN LEGION GULLETS.

The convention is posed a problem though – in the subversive form of a kitten; for the kitten will not submit, will not be framed:

but the kitten, kitten watches the
leaf fall, leaves it fall, attends to
otherwise space, its own otherwise
space, its own becoming space,
grace, cat in the green sunshine on
the kitten, on leaf

The wobbliness of the language here emphasises the uncertainty which the kitten introduces, which swells into fear ("My black guts are vacant because of this kitten") and then encourages a new, riskier perspective:

THEREFORE I RIDE OUT. I SAIL LIKE GOSSAMER.
I AM ECTOPLASM SEEKING GREEN AND TABBY SPACE.
I WILL HELP IT TO THE DARK COITUS OF MY GRID.
IT MUST BE KNOWN, THIS SPACE WHERE THE KITTEN WATCHES.

The restrictions that Conran is referring to here are analagous to those imposed by imagism which employs framing devices through the use of "superposition" (Pound's term for the placing of images on top of each other), since in this way objects define each other by contrast and so, in a sense, are located more accurately in each other's perspective – in this way it imposes defining limits on what otherwise might be intractable material. Imagism, therefore, is not merely a poetic technique, but – like the perspective grid – a way of seeing and experiencing. Its emphasis is upon limit, upon fixing boundaries that impose a sense of scale and so aid the ability to visualise. This makes it remarkably effective in some ways and frustratingly defective in others: it produces startling vividness but also tends to fix the poem statically in a rigid enclosure. A few poets have struggled with this tendency in imagism from within – the long poems of William Carlos Williams and H.D. testify to this struggle. Other poets have acknowledged the pervasiveness of its influence and used it in a radically modified form. One of the interesting features of Conran's poems – partly because he has other influences and partly because of his own view of experience as expressed in "Space" – is that they seem to be the product of an almost total immunity to imagism.

This is not to say that his poems do not employ images. What these do, however, is to indicate their own inadequacy; they do not work centripetally like images in imagist poems, bounding the poem within fixed points, but centrifugally, opening outwards. In this way the objects bestowed in his "Gift" poems, like his eponymous fern frond, accumulate meanings rather than pin them down:

> New sporelings wander the world -
> Perch high in the trees,
> Clothe banks, and float in the streams,
> Colonize screes.
>
> And Bracken rakes in his gold,
> A great tycoon,
> A subterranean emperor
> Every June
>
> Uncurling his gloved fists
>
> Even against Grass

★   ★   ★

Conran's juxtapositions have more in common with those of cubism in painting, and montage in film than they have with imagism. Here, in particular, he has much in common with other retromodernists like Edwin Morgan and Roy Fisher. He was influenced in this respect by T.S. Eliot in whom he sees a progress from the imagist "snapshots" of his first volume to the greater movement in his second:

> his technique is no longer based on the artful composition of a largely static scene in space. He is making a verbal equivalent of the motion picture ... and his new technique corresponds to what, in the world of the Cinema, they call *montage* ...

It is this technique which Conran uses in "Guernica" (Poems, 124-9). Whereas imagism characteristically employs a double perspective (one superimposed upon another), "Guernica" employs multiple perspectives − that of labourers, "barn life", Spanish fascists, German aircraft, Nature ("the sky", "the sea"), and Catholicism. Each of these poems seems, on first reading, to work metonymically through a series of displacements of images actually present in the scene. Subsequent readings, however, suggest that the whole event has been transformed in advance, for the poem is organised, at one level, around its colour symbolism which contrasts yellow and black. The black birds which stand metaphorically for the German aircraft, are opposed at some points and conspired with at others by a yellowness which stands for a natural vigour that gets perverted: "the brilliant gold of bullets"; "the sky is ripe and yellow"; "pain's undiscriminating phallus of gold". This metaphorical reading of the poem is confirmed by Conran's description of it ("Introduction", xix) as "heraldic action" − an oxymoron like "moving images", which, when applied to "Guernica", suggests that the poem is composed like a film montage assembled from armorial bearings, and indicates how the poem's elements are mediated through this controlling metaphor. This heraldic metaphor, moreover, is employed for a political end - for it helps to characterise Fascism in the way it suggests a value system, ferociously hierarchical and preoccupied with the aesthetics of violence.

   As a result the poem's self-conscious aestheticism is actually used for non- or even anti-aesthetic purposes: it refers to a state of mind which can regard the blitzing of Guernica like an author merely inventing it. In the fourth section, future mornings are compared to authors or painters with their calculating selectivity: "Blossoming mornings of winter,/ Put no face to the child that sleeps./ Put no feature, no eye or lip,/ To the body that sleeps in frost." There is a new social and historical emphasis in "Guernica" and this is combined with that self-conscious artificiality which is a feature of early Conran to indicate how human consciousness, too, is artificially constructed. This is made even more explicit in Blodeuwedd[5] in which the heroine is a character from *The Mabinogion* who was fabricated by her husband's uncle in a process that mirrors that of the poet:

> Was he my father? A point of light
> Fabricates my being. A joiner –
> A watchmaker, silversmith,
> Locksmith, cheapjack conjuror. And here I am ...
> ....
> He took the sex of meadowsweet and oaks,
> The flaming orgasm of broom, to conjure.

The death of her husband is even more artificial, even its metaphorical components being man-made:

> The death of a hero like Lleu comes in kit form.
> You have to assemble it, learn the jargon,
> Familiarise yourself with all the bits.
> Finally, you find the directions do work.
> There's a funeral to prove it.

"Guernica", too, is a poem of assembled bits - it is in this sense that it resembles montage in film and cubism in painting. The latter is an important model for its self-reflexiveness and its use of multiple viewpoint, and is even more in evidence in "Eight Answers to a Question by Paul Nicholson" (*Life Fund*, 61-65), which looks at a waterfall from eight different perspectives and is cubist in the same way as Wallace Stevens's "Thirteen Ways of Looking at a Blackbird" It uses cubism, however, in a much more social way than Stevens, and is in this respect different also from earlier, equally metaphorical Conran poems, like "Hermes", with their associative shifting between subjective worlds, where the emphasis is on what Conran himself has called an "involuted" quality, always in search of an inner centre of meaning. "Eight Answers" is metaphorical but centrifugal and takes on political meaning, referring to the "propaganda of waterfalls"; it is, moreover, even less certain that it has found the answers it set out to provide – most of them turn out to be further questions (the poem contains nine question marks).

There is a further similarity between Conran's later poems and cubism: both have an essentially modernist aesthetic which finds inspiration in pre-Renaissance art. He himself has defined the difference between contemporary Anglo-Welsh poetry and the Welsh praise-poetry that has influenced him:

> Welsh poetry, until fairly recently, was not representational art. It did not exist primarily to display a personal style or a personal point of view. It was a poetry of craftsmen. The poet was a man who had a definite job to do, part of which was to recite, or cause to be recited, his poems in public. (*The Cost of Strangeness*, 166)

More specifically, he has described the bard as

> a poet dedicated to praise, to giving honour; ultimate-
> ly to taking another person seriously, even in a non-
> intimate relationship. Bardic poetry is second-person
> poetry, an art where the *you* is more important than
> the I. (180)

It is largely, therefore, under the influence of the recited praise-
poem that Conran has written performance poems, a genre that
once again places him in a modernist tradition - the Dadaists, for
instance, especially Tristan Tzara, "would get up at public performances and would do some kind of Dadaist equivalent to
what they took to be African chanting". [6]

There are fifteen poems in *Life Fund* which are very much in
this tradition, but the idea of poetry as an activity rather than a
form of writing has had more widespread importance than this
in the later poems, which celebrate, commemorate or give praise.
In this sense these poems are, in J.L. Austin's terms, "performative" rather than "constative": (a) they do not "describe" or
"report" or constate anything at all, are not "true" or "false" and
(b) the uttering of the sentence is, or is a part of, the doing of an
action, which again would not normally be described as, or as
"just" saying something. Austin gives as examples of performa-
tives "'I name this ship *Queen Elizabeth*' - uttered when smashing
the bottle against the stern"; and "'I give and bequeath my watch
to my brother' – as occurring in a will". [7]

In this sense Conran's "Gift" poems are not 'about' the act of
giving; they dramatise the act of giving which celebrates particular occasions, and, like the examples Austin quotes, are concerned with explicitly social activity. It is partly for this reason
that, while all the "Gift" poems are centred upon an object, that
object is elaborately refused the fixedness which is essential to
imagist objects, its meaning constantly shifts; so the poet admits
in "Heron" (*Spirit Level*, 128) that he can never see the bird

Without it being
A love gift and a revelation
Of the power of all seeing.

For five seconds or so, I can stare
With my eyes clean
Of the entanglement of should be
Or ought to have been

So, too, "Upright Slate" (*Spirit Level*, 126-7) inquires into the way that objects acquire meanings, and implies that too rigid a fixing of significance upon "the natural anonymity/ Of God-given rock" requires a loss of potential. The poem, though, is ambivalent about this because, like the other "Gift" poems, it necessarily celebrates the imposition of human value on the slate, which had been carved, abandoned and then found again by someone else:

On one side only the flesh of the slate
Has been split:
Was it once the bed of a stream, this featherlike pattern
Rippling through it?

I don't even remember
Who gave it me -
Only that someone did.
Yet he or she

Liked me and it enough
To carry it home
With hands that its dead weight chilled
To the bone.

129

In the same way that "Upright Slate" inquires into the manner in which this object acquires human value, all the "Gift" poems inquire into the way that objects acquire meaning in poems, and the way that poems become centred upon objects. By reflecting upon the idea of 'given' objects (they are 'given', also, in the sense of being posited, of being stated starting-points), the poems draw attention - in the defamiliarising manner referred to by Shklovsky - to a creative artificiality in this process. The objects are necessarily arbitrary; after all it is much of the point of a gift that the object itself has self-consciously a merely surface significance - it is the "thought that counts". For this reason Conran reflects ruefully again and again on the inadequacy of the object that he is bestowing ("I'm a bit nonplussed about giving you/Such a trinket"; "An odd gift, certainly. One/Would have to be hard up/To give such a thing for a wedding.") (*Spirit Level*, 123,108).

So, by their avowed insufficiency, the images in Conran's "Gift" poems – like the controlling image in "Space" – indicate a dissatisfaction with controlling images. Instead of "expressing" a thought, and so substituting for it, the images efface themselves and defer to the thought. In this way they resist that sense of solid self-containment which characterises the imagist poem, that sense of a feeling having been thoroughly set down within defined limits. The gifts are transformed riddlingly under the gaze of the giver and deliberately withhold some of their meaning. They do not enclose a space but open one up: the space between the image and the thought that it inadequately signifies. This expressive collapse, however, increases the expressive range of the gift object because the space it opens up is one of *connotation*, of "signifying in addition" (OED). What is implied at the same time as the gift is the activity of the giver. Here Conran is connecting himself to a Welsh tradition as old as the Middle Ages, a tradition of the poet as a celebrator of human triumphs in poems given to specific individuals. As Conran himself has said

> Welsh poetry is second-person poetry. A poem prais-
> es, satirises or laments within the magnetic field of I
> and Thou. The giving and receiving of gifts, like the
> giving and receiving of poetry itself, formed the cen-
> tral arch of Welsh civilisation; and the celebration of
> gift and giver an important sub-division of the Welsh
> poetic art. (*Spirit Level*, 101)

What the gift connotes, therefore, is a poetic tradition and a social role. Where imagism frames its objects in a lyric enclosure, these gifts open outwards to imply a social meaning, for the giv-ing of such gifts is a common language and the poet shares these with his society as he shares words. The activity of giving is, as Emile Benveniste has stressed, a highly important social act: referring to the pioneering work of Marcel Mauss who "revealed the functional relationship between gift and exchange and ... defined thereby a whole group of religious, economic and judi-cial phenomena belonging to archaic societies", he goes on to demonstrate how a "vast network of rites, celebrations, contracts, and rivalries organises the mechanics of these transactions".[8]

The later Conran, then, deliberately assumes a bardic role in order to invoke social activity and the poet's traditional response to it. For this reason his poems are never relaxed with the merely lyrical: they characteristically deal with the point of intersection of the emotional with the social - with births, marriages and deaths. However, while this bardic aspect might seem another nostalgic gesture, Conran's retro-modernism constantly refuses to relapse into that kind of naiveté. His self-reflexiveness insists that his "Gift" poems are a linguistic and literary activity and that language – unlike that yearned for in an early poem like

"The Swan", but like the gifts themselves – is never entirely adequate for its occasionally being a fallen instrument. It is necessarily as a metaphor that the act of giving in the "Gift" poems condenses a number of social meanings: as the act itself, not translated into poetic language, its meaning would be much narrower. It is the metonymic element, however, of the gift itself which keeps the poem open and stops the act of giving becoming merely poetic. The gift functions "in place of", it self-consciously displaces the act of giving. It is deliberately off-centre in its arbitrariness and so decentres itself as image by deferring to the thought that counts.

So while the stress upon performance and the performative might seem to represent an attempt to acquire the authentic role of the bard, this attempt is deconstructed in order to stress both loss and continuity and allows the complexity of the poet's cultural stance to enter the poems. The poet might appear to be a man speaking to men at times, but in fact the "Gift" poems are as self-consciously fictive as *Blodeuwedd* in reconstructing the poet's role and displaying his material. The gifts themselves are, characteristically, natural objects made social - but not wholly so, since something in them remains intractably non-human. So, in "Upright Slate" he is reminded of the parent block and that "Rock's/Too much itself;/ its anonymity cries out against names". And in "Fern Frond" (*Spirit Level*, 119-22) he warns the gift's recipient, "John, don't be misled. They aren't *us*". The organic is regarded in these poems as alien and untranslatable. Society and Nature in the "Gift" poems constantly collide with each other, or slide over or under each other, but neither is allowed (to return to the terms of "Space") to frame the other, so that society gets naturalised, or Nature gets socialised. They are used, instead, as alternative perspectives which, like the cubist effects in "Guernica" and "Eight Answers", introduce defamiliarising shifts in the angle from which the subject-matter is viewed.

The poems often, therefore, show the poet in the attempt thoroughly to comprehend a natural object, but the thoroughness itself reveals the cultural aspect of the attempt. "Jasper" (*Spirit Level*, 131-3) provides a metaphor for this in the activity of "John Jones the potter" in his transformation of his material. In this way, the "gift" poems show the poetic prowess at work, enacting the movement from the natural to the artificial, and this again emphasises the movement from the natural to the artificial, and this again emphasises the constructedness of the poem.

Much of this concern is shared by another retro-modernist, Jon Silkin – born a year before Conran, in 1931 – whose "Flower Poems" compare revealingly with Conran's gifts. Silkin, like Conran, has been relentlessly concerned with how

> a hermetic or imagist art [might] be engaged with an
> art that wanted without compromising its essentiality
> to be socially orientated, involving, as it does, some
> move towards the discursive. [9]

The very marks of this anxiety in the poems of both Silkin and Conran are themselves part of the answer to it – their tendency to dwell upon images, but at the same time to fret over their insufficiency, opens cracks in the language which, as a result, continually insinuates political meaning into those images. Silkin's "Lilies of the Valley"[10], for example, keeps slipping out of imagism into a questioning that introduces registers uncomfortably inappropriate to the floral context. This is all the more effective because of the deliberate artificiality of Silkin's poetic project in this sequence, which defamiliarises flower poems as a species: a gap opens up between the flowers and the poet's treatment of them which makes the reader repeatedly aware that the vision of the flowers is that of a committed socialist and anti-Zionist Jew necessarily preoccupied with issues of justice and territory.

So the flowers and the poet's vision continually defamiliarise each other, and the same can be said of the interaction between Conran and his gifts. Silkin's flower poems, and Conran's gift poems, begin with perceptual preoccupations but their implications extend far beyond them, as they do in almost all retro-modernist poems whose authors are most accurately seen in the formalist tradition of Shklovsky as it was modified by the Futurists. As Tony Bennett has argued, for Shklovsky

> The category of defamiliarisation was ... invested with a purely aesthetic, and not with an ideological significance.
> This ran quite contrary to the position of the Futurists who viewed the devices of defamiliarisation as a means for promoting political awareness by undermining ideologically habituated modes of perception.[11]

Retro-modernist poets do not believe, as the Futurists did, that defamiliarisation can penetrate to the 'real' - but their poems keep restlessly wishing that it could, keep evolving new forms in an attempt to outwit the obstacles in the way of the real, and are always at least implicitly political in believing that stale modes of perception are "ideologically habituated". These poets keep arguing with those elements in the modern condition which fracture the self and the world and baffle the authenticity of human experience. It is for this reason that, for them, the perceptual aspects of the estrangement aesthetic are only the surface symptoms of a multi-layered activity – and the belief in depths as well as surfaces is another characteristic that distinguishes retro-modernists from postmodernists.

Notes

1. Viktor Shklovsky, *Mayakovsky and his Circle* (London: Pluto, 1974), 114.
2. Anthony Conran, *The Cost of Strangeness* (Llandysul: Gomer, 1982).
3. Anthony Conran, *Poems 1951-1967* (Denbigh, 1974), 60.
4. Anthony Conran, *Life Fund* (Llandysul: Gomer, 1979), 36-37.
5. Tony Conran, *Blodeuwedd* (Bridgend: Seren, 1989).
6. Jerome Rothenberg, "Changing the Present, Changing the Past: A New Poetics", in *Talking Poetics from the Naropa Institute*, ed. Anne Waldman and Marilyn Webb (Boulder, Colorado, 1978), 279.
7. J.L. Austin, *How to Do Things with Words* (Oxford, 1975), 5.
8. Emile Benveniste, *Problems in General Linguistics* (Coral Gables, Florida, 1971), 271.
9. Jon Silkin ed. *Poetry of the Committed Individual* (Harmondsworth: Penguin, 1973), 26.
10. Jon Silkin, *Selected Poems* (London,: Routledge, 1980), 83-84.
11. Tony Bennett, *Formalism and Marxism* (London: Methuen, 1979), 31.

"A Square of Grey Slate":
Tony Conran and Politics
Selwyn Williams

To do full justice to the depth and complexity of Tony Conran's politics, a politics inseparable from the poet and his contributions to poetry, is beyond the scope of a short essay such as this. The best that can be offered here, by focussing on one particular and memorable occasion, is a little insight into some of Tony's involvement in political activity. May the story of just one poem, "A Square of Grey Slate", written at the time of the Rhyl National Eisteddfod in 1985, serve as both tribute to and cameo of the poet, his poetry and his politics.

Over the years, Tony has been concerned with a number of cultural and political issues, both locally and nationally. He and his wife Lesley can always be counted on to turn out for events and campaigns around issues relating to Wales and the Welsh language, socialism and the peace movement, and international solidarity.

During the 1980s there was a lively socialist society in Bangor. It met regularly to debate political questions in the dank, smoky back room of an unassuming, rather seedy pub in lower High Street. One of the strengths of that society was its diversity of views and eclecticism. Its weakness was a tendency to interminable, earnest debate at the expense of practical political action. Nevertheless, there are many of us in the Bangor area, and among those who passed through at the time, who learnt much from those stimulating socialist society evenings. What a mixed bunch we were: Labour and Plaid members, CND supporters, assorted radicals, social democrats, Stalinists, Trotskyists, embryonic Greens, feminists, syndicalists, anarchists, Irish republicans, Welsh revolutionaries, Cymdeithas yr Iaith activists, non-aligned academics, Militant Tendency members, SWP cadres and more. Tony Conran was very much at home among this comradely collection of independently-minded individuals, always courteous when they espoused one-dimensional, sectarian or dogmatic views, and patient with those slow to comprehend the difference between British social imperialism and Welsh internationalism. His were invariably creative and original contributions to our fervent debates. The breadth of his intellectual framework and the depth of his human feeling and understanding fitted him for ready accommodation to the rich diversity of viewpoints which Bangor socialist society, at its best, represented. He could see "beyond the fragments" long before the fragmented began to recognise what Waldo, in the opening couplet of "Adnabod" (Recognition), calls "the disaster which lies at the hand of the analyst who loses, between his fingers, a world" (my own very rough and ready translation).

Many of us are indebted to Tony for introducing us to a rich seam of working-class ballads and poems, and for his sessions on the works of poets such as Hugh MacDiarmid and Idris Davies. When the society organised to support trade union campaigns, the miners' struggle, International Labour Day and solidarity with freedom movements in other countries Tony would always be there.

He gave his considered support to the Wales-Cuba Resource Centre (later known simply a Cymru-Cuba) in the years following the launch of this friendship and solidarity organisation at Bangor's Gŵyl Lafur (International Labour Day) in 1982.

In 1985, Cymru-Cuba, with little money, big ideas and much 'optimism of the will', decided to have a presence at the National

Eisteddfod in Rhyl, and booked a modest stall on the *maes*. To fill it, books, periodicals, newspapers, leaflets, records, cassettes, flags, badges and T-shirts were feverishly sought. Original Cymru-Cuba material was published, including commissioned articles by such writers as Tweli Griffiths, Goronwy Alun Hughes, Jan Morris, Glyn Williams, Gwyn Alf Williams and the formerly Havana-based couple Meic and Leila Haines. *Prifeirdd* Mathonwy Hughes and Gwilym R. Jones wrote *englynion* celebrating Cuba's revolution. Fringe cultural and political meetings on the *maes* were arranged, and Theatr Clwyd was hired for a major Cymru-Cuba evening of politics, music and dance. The Cuban Embassy in London promised a speaker and donated a box of first class cigars and some seven-year-old Havana Club Rum. To our delight, a few days before Eisteddfod week, Jean Stubbs, English-born wife of the well-known Cuban poet Pedro Pérez Sarduy confirmed that she and Pedro would visit the Eisteddfod on the Monday.

How best to welcome a poet of the Cuban revolution to our Eisteddfod stall? How could we convey something of Wales to Cuba? Gwilym R., unfortunately, was unwell, but Mathonwy was ready with his greetings. A copy of Tony Conran's *Penguin Book of Welsh Verse* was frantically sought, and I asked Tony to come to Rhyl to present his Penguin to Pedro.

The scene was set. Incongruously, some mischievous Eisteddfod official had positioned Cymru-Cuba's nest of revolutionaries right next door to the imposing stall of the *Cymru ar Wasgar* (the Welsh of the diaspora), which was frequented by large numbers of loud and angry United States Republicans, for whom their Eisteddfod neighbour was no more welcome than the presence of Cuba itself in Uncle Sam's 'own' back yard. Despite muted threats and mumblings about Eisteddfod rules, we held our ground - literally at times. Increasing numbers of unsuspecting *eisteddfodwyr* were caught off guard by ghetto blasts of son, salsa, rumba, conga and merengue fortified with stirring Cuban rebel and revolutionary songs. The curious stared bemused at the CYMRU-CUBA sign above the stall entrance; the timid scuttled away in the direction of the more familiar fare of *cerdd dant* or Cymdeithas Edward Llwyd. The more adventurous stepped gingerly into the revolutionary den. "What's Cuba got to do with Wales?" "Didn't know there were many Welsh in Cuba?" "Cuba's a long way away, isn't it?" Such is a sample of the less offensive remarks. A particularly hostile Pittsburgh reactionary, a third generation Welsh descendant, began to bellow; a Chilean *compañera*, a refugee from '73, muttered, just audibly, something about fat cats.

Enter, at this point, centre stage, Tony, Lesley and two lively children, wellies, raincoats, picnic and basket. Enter also, bang on cue, Jean Stubbs, two lively *niños* and Santa Clara's smiling poet-commemorator of Che Guevara, Pedro Pérez Sarduy. (The two families, incidentally, were to become good friends). Introductions and greetings followed, gifts were joyously exchanged, and a formal *bienvenidos* was extended by Cymru Cuba chair, David Jones.

In the meantime, Tony had revealed that the previous night he had just put the finishing touches to a poem he wanted to present to Pedro Sarduy. (What follows draws almost word for word on Lesley Conran's account of the making of that poem published in the trilingual volume *Adlais o America Ladin*, which was produced by the Arfon Central America group.) Apparently, Tony had doubted his suitability to take part in a presentation to a Cuban poet: he didn't speak Welsh fluently, and would therefore be breaking the most vital of Eisteddfod rules; he wrote poetry in English only; and his knowledge of modern Cuba was limited.

"Tony spent days before the Eisteddfod wandering the house and garden trying to find a suitable gift to accompany a poem to the unknown poet," wrote Lesley. "He was looking for a *llatai*, or messenger, through which to send his message, in the tradition of great Welsh poets like Dafydd ap Gwilym. The gift was finally chosen just two days before the event: a plain, rough piece of slate, such as can be found in virtually all the gardens in Bangor. The poem was inspired by that gift."

To return to that Monday morning at the Cymru-Cuba stall: out of Lesley's basket came the piece of grey slate, a copy of the poem in English and - a further contravention of Eisteddfod rules - a bottle of wine. What followed was theatre at its most moving. The *llatai* of slate was presented. A self-conscious Tony listened, head bowed, as Lesley powerfully and beautifully read out the poem, "A Square of Grey Slate", to an enthralled and privileged audience.

We were all spellbound. When Lesley came to the end of the reading, there followed a moment of silence, a fleeting stillness. Then, in an instant of true beauty, Pedro Sarduy crossed the few yards of bare earth that separated the two poets, and he and Tony embraced. We all had tears in our eyes. Our hearts ran over with joy. This was a rare moment of purity and clarity, of collective insight. Such experiences transform words like 'internationalism', 'community' and 'human love', so that they take on abidingly fresh meaning. Hope replaces scepticism.

The occasion of the presentation of that poem was for those present a powerful instance of *adnabod* (recognition). It seems to me that the poet Tony Conran's politics are, at heart, about such transforming experiences of recognition.

Thank you, Tony, for the experience of "A Square of Grey Slate". The poem ends with the line, "As the day comes on." Two politically resonant words of Welsh poetry seem an apt conclusion to this tribute, *Daw dydd* ...

One Of Our Presidents –
six variations for Tony Conran
Peter Finch

mark Conran toiler
eye bright eye old one opposite
no fish noxiousness too far inland
hook jetty over miserable history

so courteous camel eyes this man
eyes other all eyes the ones
fish leap the neat silver
riotous head who'd know they do
ox-eye, amorous, ending endless
fish our waters, hunt the new

one

old one opposite no fish noxiouness too far
inland hook jetty over miserable history so courteou
s camel eyed this man eyes other all eye

ones fish leap the neat leap the neat endl
our waters, hunt the ran toiler
bright eye old one opposite
no fish noxious
ness inland leap the neat silver
our waters, our waters,
our waters, our waters.

two

one eyed amorous endling endless
hook toiler bright old oppos
light jetty miserable neat
fish leap the fish leap the
all eyes the waters

eye bright eye old one opposite
noxiousness too far inlan
hook jet eyed this man
who'd know they do ox-eye
amorous, ending mark endless

three

Peter Finch

the toiler
mark toiler
bright eyed old toil
inland for toiling

miserable courteous neat silver
all eyes the ones fish leap
they do ox-eye toiling
hunt toiling bright toiler
mark Conran this man
bright leaping all silver

four

mk con toiler bright
neat sliver riot
us amorous ish usness
inland is nes ish rous

ish aters is man silver
endless is less endless
camel eye neat who'd know
osite rable mistory Conran
leap con who'd know us is ending
our less sliv neat eye ox endless

five

mark bright fish anxiousness
miserable miserable miserable
miserable miserable miserable
miserable who'd know

ending bright ending all eyes the ones
Conran no ending our ending
ding less amorous opposite who'd leap
hunt the neat the ones the silver
so courteous bright anxiousness
riotous camels who know the silver

six

A note on the compositional methods used for One of Our Presidents .

In an alphabet identified by the poet Jackon Mac Low (Sandra Lawrence's "The Roman Inscriptional Letter", and again in the anonymous Middle-English poem "Aristotle's ABC" letters are given specific meanings. A = ox, B = house, C = camel, and so on under Lawrence, and A = amorous, B = bold, C = courteous, etc. under Aristotle. To originate my text I allocated meanings forming the name Tony Conran, one set to each line. Line one, T for Tony, for example, gave me both "toilous" and "mark". Line two, O, gave me "eye", "opposite" and "other". Once written the piece was extended and varied using a structural process devised from Conran's poem "Blodeuwedd". The number of letters in each line of this poem were used as a process guide to my own text, with punctuation and spaces acting as direction and repeat indicators. The piece stops here at variation six although there is still plenty of fire left and one day I will carry it on.

Magical Shape-Shifting
is Almost a Way of Life:
Unstable Female Identity in
Tony Conran's *Branwen* and *Blodeuwedd*
and recent East German Drama.

Anna-Marie Taylor

Characters changing status and undergoing extraordinary transformation are distinctive components of myths and folk tales.
These stories can possess their own grammar within which the
seemingly contradictory and fanciful can be positioned to support, question and reinforce a society's laws and beliefs; a
mythologique that gives a seemingly nonsensical narrative internal
coherence[1]. The attraction of such an unconstrained mode of
story-telling is clear in Tony Conran's work for the theatre - the
stage play *Branwen* (1989, first performed by the Made in Wales
Stage Company) and the dance-poem *Blodeuwedd* (1983, exe-
cuted by Bronwen Judge and Anna Holmes) - where he consciously manipulates archaic material, skillfully presenting us
with updated recountings of *Mabinogion* stories. Above all, the
centrality of human transformation in the structure of these tales
obviously excites the author, for as Conran states in his introduction to *Blodeuwedd* [2]:

> Magical shape-shifting is almost a way of life in this
> story. Within about twenty pages we hear of stallions
> and greyhounds being made for one day out of toad-

stools; of men being made into deer and wild swine
and wolves - and both male and female ones at that;
of a girl made out of flowers; of her husband being
killed and flying away as an eagle and then spelled
back into a living man once more; and of the flower-
woman, Blodeuwedd, finally being changed into an
owl. What immediately catches our eye in this strange
tale is the superfluity of changes, the sense of the
solidity of human personality all the time dissolving
into animal forms.

Conran's vibrant description brings the early medieval tale to
life in fabulous fashion, evoking the mutability and precarious-
ness of human and animal existence. He summons up such fluidity in as richly textured and as densely inhabited a way,
although fortunately with not such grotesque menace, as a
Hieronymous Bosch canvas, with human life spilling constantly
into and out of the animal world.

Now, of course, shape-shifting is not merely confined to pre-
modern folk tales and myths, and to medieval painting. It is also
an important component of much drama and musical theatre;
witness, for example, the raw, course-vowelled Elisa Doolittle
transmuted into carefully enunciating society lady in G.B.
Shaw's *Pygmalion* (1916) and its later musical incarnation *My
Fair Lady*, gentle and harmless Galy Gay assembled into an
aggressive fighting machine in Bertolt Brecht's *Mann ist Mann*
(1926) or Hermione's 'statue' coming to life in William
Shakespeare's *The Winter's Tale* (c.1611). The fluctuating relationship between natural being and societal creation is stressed in
both *Branwen* and *Blodeuwedd*. It is no simple one, though,
above all for the way that 'the solidity of human personality dis-
solves' in these two plays makes the plays' use of archaic material
peculiarly modern and intriguing.

149

Western drama this century has depicted the 'dissolving of human personality's solidity' with great force: the dream-like states of Georg Kaiser's and August Strindberg's broken anti-heroes caught between spiritual crisis and the grubby exigencies of quotidian living; Luigi Pirandello's players on life's stage searching for authenticity; Mike Leigh's and Harold Pinter's sub-urban dwellers seeking redemption amidst the clichés and unfilled silences of cul-de-sac living; and, even more recently, the radical deconstruction of the assumed 'wholeness' of human personality, as practised by New Yorks' Wooster Group. With the exception of Strindberg, I have cited examples from countries with sizeable populations. What I should like to examine tenta-tively in this account of Tony Conran's drama is the way solidity of personality melting into air[3] (which has often been seen as one of the key features of metropolitan fictions)[4] has found particular expression in the contemporary drama of smaller, not necessari-ly metropolitan, nations.

To probe this amalgamation of individual and wider selfhood, I would like to place Tony Conran's use of shifting identity along-side two recent East(ern) German plays, *Iphigenie in Freiheit* (Iphigenia in Freedom) (1992) by Volker Braun and Manfred Karge's *Jacke wie Hose* (translated as *Man to Man*) (1982)[5], not as a postmodern collision of literatures nor for striking points of similarity in literary style, but rather for the exhilarating way that the authors have chosen to centre ideas of identity and social/national being around shape-shifting, tragic heroines.

In all four plays, the main female figure (who ranges from working-class crane-operator, to Greek priestess, battered wife, nature spirit) is seen as bearing the particular burden of nation, family or society. She is riven by the opposing demands of her position, sometimes caught between public and domestic life, sometimes between natural self and the identity conferred upon her by a wider society. On occasion she is trapped between mas-

culine authority and female subservience, and between contend-
ing political systems. This split in subjectivity might be seen, I
hope to suggest, as an apt preoccupation for writers from inter-
nally divided and contested countries.

In East(ern) Germany's case, the shape-shifting has been overwhelmingly material and geographical, brutally marked by walls,
ethnic boundaries and ideological borders, for, as T.J. Reed[6]
observes:

> ... only in Germany has the form of the nation been
> both so long delayed and so often radically undone;
> and only in German history are the break-points
> between periods so uniformly catastrophic ...

For Wales, nationhood in a modern sense has been even longer
delayed. Notions of national identity, shared statehood and civic
selfhood have (thankfully) been far less fixed than in Germany.
But, for those intent on defining 'Wales' and 'Welshness', such
lack of consensus has made the whole national debate frustratingly (and also fascinatingly) fluid.[7]

Perhaps, after such nebulous talk, I should begin with the earliest
and least ambiguous treatment of magical shape-shifting, Manfred
Karge's *Jacke wie Hose*, where, without any equivocation, the
author sets out to depict the effect of 'the break-points between
periods' on individual and mass behaviour. The dramatist himself
was used to profound re-adjustment: born in East Germany and
trained as a writer/director at the Berliner Ensemble, Karge wrote
this play when he had crossed the border between Germanies to
work in the Federal Republic at the Bochum Staatstheater. Edgar
Reitz's impressive series of films *Heimat* (Home) (1985), presents
a central female figure through and around whom both a personal
story of German survival this century and a wider account of
German historical identity can be narrated. Reitz chooses the

country-dweller Maria as his national representative. Born in 1900 into rural Hunsruck on the western margins of the German Reich, Maria, a benign and all-forgiving mother figure, acts mainly as silent witness to the wider scale and catastrophic changes to her extended family, home village and nation. In contrast to Reitz's expansive and overwhelmingly humane view of how the personal history of people without power can intersect with a wider political history, and how compassion can survive against the odds, Karge writes from a different German perspective, abrasively shearing and pruning dramatic monologue to grotesque effect in order to show how brutally imposed political systems have grossly distorted German behaviour.

Karge uses the true story of a woman who took on her husband's identity and job (in the play as a crane-driver) after his death to survive during the German depression of the 1920s. He appropriates "the breeches' parts not for erotic ... but ... for social purposes".[8] Such an extraordinary transformation and change of status are not used as a pathological individual case-study, but rather act as a highly concrete expression of the various shifts in identity forced on Germans this century. The differing regimes are seen as overbearingly authoritarian and masculine in their values.

Ella's initiation into German masculinity is every bit as dark as any primitive ritual, her female self cast off and reassembled in strange and stomach-churning rites, where German manhood is celebrated in card playing, beer and pickled pork consumption:

> Put your cards on the table, Max. A queen.
> Faint hearts ne'er won fair lady. Diamonds are a girl's
> best friend. My head is spinning
> And beer and schnapps all churned up together
> And schnapps and beer and fill them up again.
> A man's gut don't easily call it a day.

BEER WOMAN HERE WOMAN BEER BEER BEER
BEER
And with the next round they order pickled leg of pork,
With onions, peas and mustard on the side.
No pork? What's up? Not kosher?
Bet you're circumcised. Bet you're not called Max
Gericke at all, but Nathan Rosenberg.
And two fine specimens of German manhood rise,
Tottering, to their feet. Eat or die.
... I wave the bones in triumph once I've done -
Then bawl out; ICH BIN EIN DEUTSCHER MANN! [9]

This moment of triumphant, if repugnant, transformation in the
late Weimar years into true-born German male marks Ella's passage from female to male. There is no going back – economic
survival determines all, as Ella/Max relates:

The plan is: I'll slip back into her skin,
Take off my suit, unknot my tie,
And take refuge in a blouse and skirt.
And what's to become of him, the man I am?
And me? The woman I want to be?
I think myself back and I think myself forward.
Who? Where, when, how come I got like this?
.... The clock strikes five. It's time to wear the trousers. [10]

Karge's adroit fusion of first and third person narration, and
constant movement between confessional directness to objective
reportage of circumstances, between sentimentality and harsh
realism, further reinforces the sense of Ella/Max's oscillating
identity being not part of a personal study but also standing in
for the truncated development of modern Germany as a whole,
from Kaiser to Weimar to Hitler to divided territory.

153

Genuine expression of feelings is denied to Ella the man, extremes of emotion occasionally sanctioned as lachrymose sentimentality. In her only heroic moment, Ella renounces her female self entirely when she gives her identity papers to Puppchen the canteen lady who is besotted with the 'man' Max. Puppchen is involved in left-wing politics and by becoming Ella Gericke she can escape from Hitler's Germany, another passing on and shifting of identity in this story.

Karge's play, described by the author as "a life of Germany in monologue form, reflecting the last few decades of German history", uses its central figure unashamedly as allegorical of her/his nation's(s') progress. When we place Conran's *Branwen* alongside it, it is apparent that Conran's treatment of the *Mabinogion* tale also inhabits a public domain; although its political meanings are not articulated as overtly and neatly as in *Jacke wie Hose*. As with so much of his poetry (fine examples being "Elegy for the Welsh Dead, in the Falkland Islands, 1982" and "A Square of Grey Slate"), Tony Conran's especial strength in *Branwen* is the manner in which he has fused past and present. Here the curious and unsettling chronicle of kingdoms sealed and lost around a debased wife, mutilated horses, unreasonable punishment, and a sacrificed child is allowed to articulate contemporary political issues. Conran accommodates the weird mytho-logic of the original, in which there seems to be a submerged text dealing with the kinship and parenthood of early British territories, and, without deviating far from the *Mabinogion* material, he creates a futuristic Celtic world of juntas, authoritarianism and revolutionary causes shaped within present Brito-Irish relations.

The different time-scales in the play – archaic time (summoned up in the semi-mythical origins of the characters, the early modern locations such as the Royal Court at Aberffraw, deliberately anachronistic folk songs, lyric poems and riddles), the present political reality of divided Ireland (and Wales), and largely imagined future world of state terror – make this play particularly resonant, rich in associations and multifarious in its meanings. Is *Branwen*, for example, a play about past relations between Wales and Ireland?, the impossibility of pan-Celtic understanding?, the limitations of revolution?, dynastic rivalries in a large politically ruthless family?, present-day reporting of political events?, the abuse of female rights?, or is this "revolutionary tragedy" about all these things simultaneously? What is certain is that these various meanings are overwhelmingly articulated through and acted out upon the central female figure, who, like Ella/Max is broken down and subject to radical shifts in identity throughout the play.

As opposed to other retellings of the tale, Branwen here is not mute and passive. She rebels publicly against her marriage to Matholwch, King of Ireland, seeing her own identity and autonomy as subordinate to her brother Brân leader of the Revolution's desire to "have an alliance with the greatest power in the west! ... the King of the Picts (will not) waste ... good money trying to de-stabilize us".[11] Branwen's manner of rebelling is extreme, revealing her as the vehicle through which the Irish/British territories will be procreated and joined dynastically:

> "It's a big womb I have, is it? Breasts, look at them,
> They'll suckle his brats."

In order to disassociate herself from the power-mongering of her brothers and their camps, Branwen dresses herself as a tinker, denuding herself of previous social elevation. The language of her denial sounds almost Biblical, a casting of herself into the wilderness:

Brian Tarr

*Eilian Wyn as Manawydan in the Made in Wales production of **Branwen**, 1989.*

Let my body go cold in the wind,
Let my feet go yellow with dust,
Let me eat roots.

The scouring frost burnish my hands,
Skin of my legs torn by bramble,
My bed the leaves under a hedge.

Let me be tinker again. A beggar girl.

This particular transformation, allows the central female pro-
tagonist to see the world she is innocent of, the human chaos that
various militaristic groups have created. This levelling down, an
extinction of her privileged identity, brings Branwen into contact
with the fears and terror unleashed by the revolution, giving her
a pivotal position in the play as the bridge between several communities, between the people of Britain and those in power,
between "the two third-world countries" of Ireland and Britain
(and quite likely in production between audience and stage
action).

Branwen's abnegation of power and privilege is echoed ironically after the alliance between Brân's country and Ireland has
been sealed with her marriage. The physical punishment of
Branwen by Matholwch, and her descent at court to work as
kitchen maid, marks a savage transformation in her status. Here
inter-Celtic animosities are made concrete, and acted out upon
the broken down, bruised woman, whose unjust debasement
within Conran's play is linked, not just structurally but themati-
cally, to the violation of the king's horses by her half-brother.
Animals, peasants and queens are the weak within the authoritarian politics of the Island of the Mighty. The final violation and
transformation of Branwen into childless mother, when her child
Gwern is flung onto the fire by her half-brother Efnisien, con-

157

firms such brutality, bringing together, within the vacillating time-scales of the play, the savage reality of Wales's too often romanticised Celtic past, as well as our uncivilised historical present, and the imagined terror and political violence of Conran's Third World future.

Branwen is a complex play, with its meanings caught between past, present and futuristic visions of Brito-Irish relations. The accommodation of the original's non-psychological treatment of human motivation also makes the text sometimes difficult to envisage, although conversely vitally non-naturalistic, almost ceremonial, in performance. Unlike Ceri Sherlock's more realistic film *Branwen* (1994), based on Gareth Miles's *Dyrnod Branwen* (Branwen's Blows), which also took on present-day Welsh-Irish relations, Conran's play makes little attempt to plug the unspoken gaps with psychological realism. Much in Conran's play remains, like the *Mabinogion* original, unresolved and puzzling, giving perhaps the impression that (Welsh) selfhood is liminal and never stable, to be constantly negotiated between different states, both political and personal. The final and only point of stability is that of Branwen's brother Manawydan, guardian of his sister's (and her country's?) tragic history, Candidean in his desire to withdraw himself from political action, resigned not to tending his garden but to cobbling shoes.

If we move on to Volker Braun's *Iphigenie in Freiheit*, here all is liminal, as the figure caught up in change is betwixt and between complex political break-points. Newly freed Iphigenia speaks for her dying nation, representing as she does East Germans' feelings of complete bewilderment, as they collide headlong with Western capitalism. Taking "the curious time after the breakdown of East Germany, when the German Democratic Republic still existed but wasn't, and when the Federal Republic did not quite exist but already did"[12], Braun turns to the figure of Iphigenia, who has served in religious isolation after the slaughter of her father Agamemnon. Through her plight he expresses his disquieted puzzlement at the demise of his country. Iphigenia's prior incarceration is linked to the land-locked and sometimes imprisoned position of former East Germans up to 1989. Such bewilderment expressed through Agamemnon's daughter is not only Braun's. The striking feature of this play is the way that author, former nation (is it independent now or has it become a colony?) and the mythical figure are fused. The author, whose role in East Germany was as supporter of socialist principles but frequent critic of the regime, does not absent himself from the text, ironically commenting from within in Orestes/Electra's opening speech:

> DAS VOLK/
> Ich bin Volker [13]   (The folk, I am Volker),

conjuring up a whole fractured history of German nationhoods with the different applications of 'Volk' [14].

The dissolution of the whole state is made tangible in the writing of the play where there is not only leakage between author and text, but, as with Orestes and Electra, between characters within the play. The whole effect of the piece is to encapsulate the sense of a political system with its previous linguistic connotations and societal affiliations breaking up and spinning out of control. Words and lived experience in the GDR are now empty signifiers to many in the new Germany, and Iphigenia in her newly given freedom undergoes a radical onslaught on her previous GDR self. This attack on her identity comes not only from her helplessness in a newly commercialised world where 'out of town shopping cemeteries' [15] are to be negotiated, and where she has lost her power, disarmed by advertising. The demi-goddess is also terrorised by her family's/nation's past; which, in its dreadful bloodshed, recalls the cursed House of Atreus:

159

"What kind of family is this? MURDERER-FATHER
MURDERER-MOTHER MOTHER-MURDERER. [16]

No emotion of Iphigenia's or her generation's is pure, influenced
as they are by present and past. Iphigenia's homesickness, for
example, is not just for the reality of former East Germany, but
also for a past before the catastrophic and bloody events of this
century – "We want our Kaiser back".[17] No German here can
live without traces of the past being evident, whether it be in
desiring, hating or even shopping in a supermarket, where, in
this high-pitched lament of a play, the out of town development
is linked to Ravensbruck concentration camp. The present day
dissonance of emotions recalls a previous Iphigenia by crass contrast, an Iphigenia before the storm of history broke, Goethe's
Iphigenie auf Tauris (1787). The eighteenth-century figure represented grace, serenity and enlightenment, ideals of humanity – a
bitter contrast to Braun's out of control, desperately lost and
uncertain representative of the 1990s.

Dissolution of self is also prominent in Conran's remarkable
dance-poem *Blodeuwedd*, which, like Karge's and Braun's play,
articulates complicated ideas about self (and, to a lesser degree,
nation) through vacillating female identity. As with *Branwen*,
Conran has stayed close to the original tale, casting the ancient
story, however, in a contemporary framework of reference.
Blodeuwedd is related entirely by Gwydion's beautiful creation,
the flower-woman, made for the magician's son Lleu, in a striking and technically daring montage of different forms of address.
These range from direct expression of feelings (usually of loss
and anger):

> I was never by him given a childhood.
> No one prospected my gibberish for words –
> Mam mam, mam mam – or held their arms
> For my first free steps. He never thought of it.[18],

to objective telling of facts:

> The police say that the Chief Inspector
> Recovered my husband's body actually alive.
> They say despite severe wounds, malnutrition,
> Shock and weakness, Lleu lives. [19],

to Conran's beloved riddling:

> Where was the Sow born?
> Under the hill. Under the hill.
> How many in the litter?
> Twelve and twelve. Twelve and twelve. [20]

The dramatic poem also accommodates glorious passages of nature description where, like Caliban, Blodeuwedd reveals herself to be highly cognisant of the natural world – of plants, animals, physical sensations – of which she is part. Conran is marvellously skilled at evoking her animalistic self. Blodeuwedd here is much more animal-like in her responses than Saunders Lewis's divided heroine. The assault on her husband (by her lover) is recorded with the cool gaze of a stalking beast:

> ... He was laughing
> When the enormous spear gutted him.
> ... I was so near I saw the sky explode out of his eyes. [21]

and the sexual encounters of this 'counterfeit woman' with her husband are anatomised with curious frigidity:

> I feel his swollen tube warm against my crotch.
> I touch it with my long fingers. We move together.
> My husband jerks inside me, moves, moves, moves. [22]

Such cold distance is in sharp contrast to her instinctual response to a hunted stag:

> My thighs stiffen, my head rotates.
> I look for the hunter, smile
> To his insolent salute. He will kill,
>
> ... I have a sudden hunger for meat.[23]

This affinity with the earth and her non-human, conscience-less response to pain, lust and murder make the levelling down of Blodeuwedd to admiring and dutiful wife close to comic:

> My husband Lleu is a great man around town.
> He has top people for friends. Apparently
> They like me ...
> They think me suitable for Lleu.
> My beauty decorates their admiration for him. [24]

Such Stepford Wife-like submission to Lleu highlights the tragic isolation of her creation. Blodeuwedd is different, special, and, like Lulu in Wedekind's *Earth Spirit* (1895) who also exists for men's desires, she cannot be tied down to everyday life and needs. Her tragedy, though, is that to be partly human she has to commit an act of transgression by having her own sexual desires, by desiring Gronw Bebyr.

Blodeuwedd's desire for Gronw is left oddly unstated in Conran's poem (covered mainly in her bloodthirsty response to his hunting), although the invasion of Blodeuwedd's body by his child is described graphically in both repulsed and fascinated terms:

> And for months after I would dream the birth -
> I who had never borne baby, dreamt it
> To the last detail. ...
> Roll over like an egg, lose nose and eyes,
> And wait for my warmth to hatch it. [25]

Here the transformation of Blodeuwedd into mother is resisted as unnatural; the creature "begotten in the lure of bees" and "bastard of mead and moorland" [26] trespassed upon by human flesh.

The maternal transformation fails to take place, and the narrative drive of the poem moves to the final transformation of Blodeuwedd into bird of the night. As the poem reaches its end, there is a palpable and striking change in Blodeuwedd's emotional state, as if human feelings are breaking through as her body shrinks into the owl's skeleton:

> I have killed his son. Grief
> Is the name and bent of the fable. [27]

With this change in emotional register, Conran's poem opens up questions about Blodeuwedd's identity. Is the figure relating the tale human (not a magical creation) but lacking "an emotional structure to make her human" [28], an interpretation offered by the author of this strange tale of transformation? Is "this a poem about a girl going insane, becoming an owl, a thing of darkness"[29]? Are we invited to share the psychology of a personality falling apart, and inhabiting human feelings and actions that could be interpreted as insane? Certainly, her attempted drowning in the lake is accompanied by what seem to be crazed visions of

> ... a devastation
> Naked to the air. And with them, the dead
> Bodies of girls float or strew the shore.
> Enid, her frock bunched up to her shoulders,
> Shows a cleft rump to the morning. Eigr,
> Once with green eyes, is attended to
> By an assiduous crow. Elen and Luned
> Grind pretty noses to the merciless stone.[29]

This legion of dead girls, presumably suicides, possibly victims of violence, however, pushes the meaning of *Blodeuwedd* in a different direction; placing Blodeuwedd's social dysfunction in a less solipsistic context. The poem sequence changes into a dance of death; death of youthful hopes, death of a son, death of a beautiful flower woman turned into "a pathetic, dumpy heap,/ Of dowdy feathers" [30] – a world of destruction, aggression and horror that flickers at the edges of Blodeuwedd's tale.

As with the other plays I have discussed, the power of this dramatic piece lies in Conran's ability to evoke several realities at once, a shifting unstable form of narration, where there is the sense of various worlds (social, historical, familial, mythical and personal) co-inhabiting the story. I am conscious that I have touched upon a number of wide areas of discussion, and have tossed terms such as 'nation', 'myth', 'motherhood', 'identity' around like Lottery balls (to use a banal, unConran-like, and distinctly unarchaic simile), waiting for the words to fall into a winning formula. But I am no Gwydion, and transmuting my observations into a grand narrative of nation and narration would need much further study of the drama of smaller nations. However, I should like to conclude by suggesting that the plays discussed here are remarkable for the way that they have extended and manipulated dramatic form, providing the means to express not only the fluidity of human personality but also an apprehension of living in countries that "shape-shift almost as a way of life".

Notes

1. As meticulously, if programmatically, put forward in Claude Levi-Strauss *Mythologiques,* 4 vols, Paris, 1964-72; the first two volumes translated as *The Raw and the Cooked* and *From Honey to Ashes,* translated by J. and D. Weightmann, London and New York, 1969 and 1973.

2. Tony Conran (1988) *Blodeuwedd and other poems* (Ogmore-by Sea; Poetry Wales Press), 66-67.

3. To conflate Tony Conran and Marshall Berman's appropriation of Karl Marx's description of modernity as 'all that is solid melts into air' for the title of his discussion of modernisation (London, 1983). My apologies for this complicating inter-textuality!

4. This is certainly the case in many discussions of Modernism which is seen as largely having taken place in large metropolitan centres such as Berlin, Moscow, Paris and London.

5. Translated very well by Anthony Vivis (1988) as *Man to Man* (London: Methuen).

6. T. J. Reed "Another Piece of the Past: Writing since the Wende" in Axel Goodbody and Dennis Tate (eds) (1992), *Geist and Macht, Writers and State in the GDR*, (Amsterdam/Atlanta: Rodopi), 215.

7. For example, Dai Smith (1984) *Wales! Wales?* (London: Allen and Unwin) and Gwyn A. Williams (1985) *When was Wales?* (Reading: Penguin).

8. *Vivis op. cit.,* 45.

9. *Ibid.,* 33-4.

10. *Ibid.,* 36.

11. I quote from the acting version, aware that a published text may be different.

12. Introduction to Volker Braun (1992) *Iphigenie in Freiheit,* Frankfurt am Main: Suhrkamp.

13. Braun, op. cit., 7 (my translations).

14. Including the Nazi state's racialist application and the revolutionary use of a 'Volk' united against the regime in East Germany's final days, 1988-89.

15. Braun, *op. cit.* 27.

16. Braun, *op. cit.* 9.

17. Braun, *op. cit.* 28.

18. Conran, *Blodeuwedd,* op. cit. 39

19. Conran, *op. cit.* 55.

20. Conran, *op. cit.* 52.
21. Conran, *op. cit.* 47.
22. Conran, *op. cit.* 42.
23. Conran, *op. cit.* 43.
24. Conran, *op. cit.* 41.
25. Conran, *op. cit.* 57.
26. Conran, *op. cit.* 38.
27. Conran, *op. cit.* 67.
28. *Ibid.*
29. Conran, *op. cit.* 63.
30. Conran, *op. cit.* 65.

Brian Tarr

The cast of **Branwen.**

Working with the Dramatist

Gilly Adams

My *Branwen* file reveals a sheaf of letters, photographs and press cuttings. Somewhere in the back a rehearsal schedule sticks out, reminder of the stress of doing extraordinarily difficult things in a very short time. I look in the appropriate boxes for the script and find several different versions - the most familiar lurks in a battered black folder with my name on the front. This is the version we used for production in 1989. *Branwen*, A Revolutionary Tragedy, by Tony Conran, the grubby front page announces; this was the third 'version' of the play and there is evidence of continuing work in rehearsal in the re-pasted pages which appear now and then in the script. In other boxes I find the texts which preceded and succeeded this performed version, some I distinguish by their covers or the particular typeface. A later model is annotated "Cardiff Literature Festival" in deference to the last public reading of the play in 1990.

I flick through the pages of 'my' script and lines flash out at me bringing in their train a kaleidoscope of images which take that particular sequence of words on the transformative journey from the rehearsal room to the stage. I leaf through the letters - ten years' worth of correspondence - and find in the thick wodges of paper from the earlier years evidence of that frustrating thing, 'the dramaturgical process', the extended dialogue between writer and director which changes a play from words written in isolation into a theatrical event, a collaboration of many talents, a communication with an audience. Intrigued, I sit down to read the letters again. Tony's are often lengthy, words crammed into the margins of pages which have been turned around in the typewriter to maximise every inch of paper, occasionally annotated in his spidery writing, always signed "in love and joy" however much we disagree. Mine are shorter, on the headed notepaper of the Made in Wales Stage Company, sometimes typed formally (anything to do with money is typed) sometimes written in my how-many-words-can-I-cram-into-a-line script.

Differences in paper and presentation reflect the passage of time from the beginnings of our mutual engagement with *Branwen* in the drama studio of the Drama Department in Bangor university, where we tested the embryonic play with student actors who willed us to entertain them, to the full professional production in the Studio at Theatr Clwyd and on to the subsequent readings at the Edinburgh Festival and in Cardiff.

In one of Tony's letters (27/6/86) I have marked several lines boldly in felt-tip pen:

> For the last three years I think I have been so impressed with feminism that I've been in danger of over-identifying with women.

For me, as a woman director working in the male world of Welsh theatre, this was an exciting and welcome statement which was reinforced by Tony's portrayal of Branwen in his play. The principal women in *The Mabinogion* - Rhiannon, Branwen, Blodeuwedd - are passive, almost mute. Prior to *Branwen* Tony had written a long poem for dancer/performers about Blodeuwedd which he described as "the psychological, mythical, magical poetic response to a woman's predicament in a feminist crossfire". In *Branwen*, he goes further in creating a woman who is "concerned to preserve her feminine integrity in a revolution in which she has played her part." And it's true: this retelling of

168

the old Celtic story puts Branwen centre stage by exploring her emotional and political journey and the consequences of her actions. "Branwen is not at all counterfeit," he wrote in the same letter. "The decisions she makes are her own, however limited by men's expectations of her."

So, an important Welsh play with a woman at its heart and an exhilarating fusion of glorious language, folk song and dance. (more of this later - here lies contention.) From the outset Tony saw in the ancient story elements of the contemporary world: domestic violence, dynastic marriage, atrocity and appeasement, even holocaust, and he was not prepared to let his audience escape into a kind of medieval never-never land. In an interview with Greg Hill in *Bilingual Matters*, (Spring 1991) he states:

> Tragedy is about now, but its method of dealing with it is metaphorical. The tragic world, like a miracle play, is fundamentally anachronistic . . . it lives in its own time, tangential to all our worlds.

In Tony's interpretation of *Branwen*, epic history is made contemporary by setting the action in neighbouring Third World countries: Ancient Britain and the Kingdom of Ireland. The thrilling opening takes us from the individual voices of Branwen and Manawydan reflecting on family history to the full-throated roar of the Revolution. Brân is the Revolutionary leader whose forces have defeated the junta (General-in-Chief Euroswydd) as the play begins. Brân becomes king ("the yellow gold is round his feet") and, without consultation, Branwen is offered to the Irish king.

> No, my fine brother. You make me a whore
> The Irishman fancies my cunt.

169

Although she consents to marry Matholwch for political reasons, Branwen's personal tragedy is set in motion and many others go with her:

> 'I am a curse to the world, she cried.
> 'Two good islands
> Have been destroyed because of me'.

Efnisien's psychotic intervention is not minimised but Tony gives him an acute and troubling intelligence which analyses Brân's behaviour and finds it wanting:

> Well, you're a fool. You destroyed Branwen
> For your fucking Revolution.
> Now you've ditched the Revolution for her.

– and Nisien emerges as the loving innocent, the skylark, whose death escaping from Ireland after visiting Branwen in secret begins the breaking of her heart. Tony reminds us that "tragedy is about now" with devices like sharply anachronistic radio broadcasts but also in lines which are shocking in their immediacy such as Branwen's description of the Irish situation:

> Reprisal. Atrocity. Desperation.
> It could go on for years . . .
>
> . . . Road block and crying child
>
> The slit of a knock on the door -
> The peculiar walk of soldiers
> When they know they are vulnerable.

The freshness of Tony's vision in tandem with the demands of the epic story were enormously challenging. His text left plenty of space for the theatrical imagination to breathe. How do you cremate a baby, carry out an ambush, and suggest the devastation of a holocaust with scant resources, and all within about five minutes? Such is the stuff of invention and practice, as was the need to master the use of verse as the language base of the play. Early in rehearsals Tony lectured the company on the complexities of medieval Welsh verse, explaining that the "saga-poems" such as "Stafell Gynddylan" were dialogues written in three-line stanzas of varying shapes and that he had used this as the basis for dialogue in *Branwen* with the addition of some lyrical passages, songs and simple line alternations. For us, the beauty and power of the language was a constant delight and Tony wrote to me much later:

> I still think that some of the poetic bits are a bit of a self indulgence, but one of the things I have learned in our disputes and re-writings is that genuinely dramatic poetry - tragic poetry - is in fact the most dramatic thing you can have.

Whilst we were able to reach agreement about much of the text, the real area of dispute between us was the morris dance which Tony had integrated carefully into the original play as a metaphor for the ritual of community and a means of dancing the Revolution. He meticulously researched and selected appropriate dances and folk songs, and patterned them into an intricate structure with the verse (all this is wonderfully analysed in a huge letter which he wrote to me in May 1987), but after various experiments with this form (chiefly with the students in Bangor where we all took morris-dancing lessons), I became convinced that the morris was holding the play back and that a different theatrical metaphor for Revolution would liberate the text. For me, the problem was partly the familiar one of the writer neither being able to envisage the real theatrical potential of what he had written nor being able to let go of it. It was also a matter of economics. The employment of eight actors and two musicians was lavish in the context of Made in Wales's usual budgets - an additional team of dancers would have prohibited a production. We wrangled back and fore - cajoling, persuading, demonstrating - and finally I wrote to him in July 1988 offering a commission for *Branwen* for a production in the following year without morris but with actors who could sing and dance, and the important contribution of a composer and a choreographer. We tested this way of delivering the text in a rehearsed reading in the *Write On* Festival in November 1988 after which Tony conceded in a letter that he was finding the morris convention unfinishable, although he had found it so hard to imagine the play without it; but he could now envisage a morris-less version of *Branwen* as a "fast moving 'classical' verse tragedy which preserves . . . the unity of action, focused solidly on the five siblings but bearing on the Revolution theme also." We had found a way forward together (without which *Branwen* would never have been produced) and I remain convinced that we made the right decision in terms of theatrical impact; but for Tony, I think, an ambiguity remains. In an interview in early 1991 he said:

> ... essentially it was a translation job into a somewhat different kind of theatre to what I'd envisaged. But that is the nature of the game. She did most of the work of translating, and made a great go of it. I learnt a hell of a lot.

But in a letter to me in May of the same year, about the difficulty of getting the play published, he wrote:

> The trouble is both my original failure to see the play through in terms of morris, and your determination (or whatever) to produce it without morris, have introduced a warp in the very heart of the play as an integrated concept.

Whatever the difficulties along the way, the production was a success and the play considered significant. We retained the figure of the Cadi from the morris version as a kind of Everyperson and Lady of Misrule, linking the audience with the action, and the focus of the production style was the ensemble of actors coming together to tell the story. Rona Lee, the designer, immediately grasped Tony's desire for a mixture of the timeless and the now, and the two images which she used as a starting point for her design acknowledged this: Tibetan prayer flags fluttering in the breeze and, in total contrast, a picture of a woman in a white evening dress holding a young girl by the hand walking away from us along a curved motorway beneath urban lights. Her final set used lengths of wood in a configuration which suggested both telegraph poles and forest, and which culminated in a crow's-nest. Phil Thomas, the composer, worked carefully with Tony's original selection of folk songs, orchestrated them for voices and cello, and added some original music of his own which was complex and enthralling.

Some powerful memories/images of the production come back to me:

- the relief in the technical rehearsal when the 'holocaust' worked for the first time (thank you, Theatr Clwyd technicians);

- Amanda Wright's vulnerability, head thrown back, neck exposed, in Branwen's exquisite lament for the death of Nisien:

> Brother, how will Efnisien
> Find home now, for the dark
> Has taken you, my man, my skylark?

- the young black actress, Rakie Ayola, singing about "the deadly wars" in a moment of great solemnity;

- the gasp of horror from the first-night audience when the roll of material that made up the "baby" unfurled into the fire;

- the flock of black birds that rose magically into the twilight as if on cue at an open-air performance at the Bishop's Palace in St. David's;

- bursting into tears of relief after the first performance when Tony hugged me and said he was pleased with the production.

For all of us, it was a special time and the reviews reflected that feeling. *The Guardian's* critic said that "Conran's writing somehow combined a language that is not archaic but up-to-date as the News at Ten with high flown poetic imagery", and he was "bewitched by the theatrical wizardry"; *The Independent* commented that "Heroism is clearly still made in Wales". Most satisfyingly, Radio 4's *Kaleidoscope* programme commented on the play's "speaking beyond the theatre walls and addressing the nation as a whole".

Ironically, despite such critical attention and subsequent efforts to organise another tour, *Branwen* has never received the second production it deserved and hence has never been seen in Cardiff, which leaves me with a sense of incompleteness. Tony's subsequent plays have remained fragmentary and elusive in dramatic terms, and confirm my fundamental sense that he is a poet first and a playwright second. But in *Branwen* he gave us perhaps the best play of the last decade - a play which is an allegory for what he himself described as the "heroic failure" of being Welsh, a play which feeds our hunger to be retold our past in a way that illuminates the present.

A final image from the rehearsal room. Tony Conran, poet and playwright, sitting apart from the action, silent and absorbed, a strong presence. Somehow this chimes with a paradox central to *Branwen*. Brân, the revolutionary leader, the Black Crow, the tragic hero, is never seen, never participates, but his brooding presence is at the heart of the story which unfolds.

Constructing Community:
Tony Conran's *Castles*

Tony Brown

Over twenty years ago, Tony Conran ended his autobiographical essay in the *Artists in Wales* series by comparing the "great impersonal opportunities" of the Welsh praise tradition with what he sees as the English pattern, where the poet writes directly out of his personal experience: "The poet uses his individual experience as raw material; he processes this with his art, and turns it into poems, commodities which he puts up for sale, first in magazines and then in books".[1] This latter tradition, he argues, is dying in a world in which individual experience is becoming less and less significant ("in modern physics, in ecology, in advanced psychotherapy, the impossibility of remaining a detached observer, a 'point of view', has been amply demonstrated"); our educational system, though, still teaches our children the value of being individuals and it is this "monopoly culture we call 'education'" which helps keep alive the tradition of the direct expression of individual experience: "The art of self-expression, poetry itself, is rapidly becoming an educational appendage". The alternatives to this mode of poetry, the alternatives which Tony Conran sees as being more suited to our own fragmented society, are the impersonal modes, first, of the Welsh praise tradition, which expressed community rather than the poet's individuality, and, second, the Modernist tradition, which instead of the single point-of-view expresses the complex, multi-faceted nature of our world: "Perhaps this is why poets like David Jones or Basil

Bunting or the Pound of the *Cantos* still keep the respect of the real poetry-reading public. You try teaching Pound's *Cantos* to a group of sixth-formers, let alone fourth-formers!" (*Artists,* 123). Some twenty years later, in a characteristically trenchant essay on "Modernism in Anglo Welsh Poetry", Conran's attack is strikingly similar, though more precisely-focussed. He notes that "if there is any profession that preponderates in the so-called 'Second Flowering' [of Anglo-Welsh poetry] it is the teachers, including ... lecturers at training colleges and inspectors of schools"[2]. The poetry produced by this "pedagocracy", he argues, is

> Without exception ... unmodernist. [The poets] hard-
> ly experiment with form in any significant way. They
> establish a single perspective and stick to it. The
> poems are recognisably about something, in the way
> that a representational picture is about a landscape or
> an experience. They rarely 'aspire to the condition of
> music'.[3]

Again, such a poetry of the single, subjective, point-of-view is inadequate: "Our culture is profoundly schizoid, and to pretend it is not — to build poems as though we were capable of single and unique points of view — is to cut ourselves off from our reality". Earlier in the essay, Conran draws attention to a poem by Davies Aberpennar, "Poem for M.A.J.D.", included in Keidrych Rhys's *Modern Welsh Poetry* (1944):

> [T]he train of thought is, to say the least, oblique. The
> assumption is certainly not that poetry ought to be
> available to English pupils in a sixth form. Modernism
> is taken for granted in this poem, shown by its difficul-
> ty, its multiple perspective (as in a Cubist painting), its

use of the culture of the past as both palimpsest and template, and its genuine attempt to use free verse as an expression of modern sensibility.

In almost every respect this description can also be applied to Tony Conran's *Castles*.[5] Distinctively Welsh in its concerns, its field of reference and in some of its verse forms, it is also decisively Modernist in its techniques, dense and allusive; its refusal of a single viewpoint, its complex intercutting of the personal with mythic and historical material, calls to mind Geoffrey Hill's *Mercian Hymns* (1971) and Basil Bunting's magnificent *Briggflatts* (1966), although that is not to suggest indebtedness but a measure of the poem's achievement.[6] It is at the same time, for all its occasional obliqueness and difficulty, "about something"; indeed it is about many things, to the extent that to attempt a linear discussion of the poem is a daunting task. *Castles* is about power and the vulnerability of power, about Wales, her history and her present condition; it is about the power of language and the function of poetry; it is about the way we construct ourselves and try to make a home for ourselves in the world, and about the vulnerability of all our creative acts in the face of natural process and the flux of time. The central thematic tension, multi-layered as it is, is announced in a "Note" at the beginning of the poem:

An earl builds a castle, a viking inscribes a rune on a stone, an artist paints a picture ... The act is one of assertion, of class-power or personal aggrandisement. To make it we have to destroy or wound unwillable things — trees, communities, the flow of the world, loving. That is the first part of the Theme. But then the assertion fails, the castle is ruined, the civilization collapses. Into the gap flood back the non-assertive,

178

the inhuman, the subconscious — death, trees, fear, religion, what might have been. That is the second part of the Theme.

All the variations are on this Theme, either as a whole or on one or other part of it: but even where only one part is explicit, the other must be felt as implied. 'Theme' is used here in a musical sense, not necessarily to describe what either the sections or the poem as a whole is about.[7]

It is, consciously, then a poem that, in its formal organisation, "aspire[s] to the condition of music", a set of variations; in an unpublished "Commentary and Meditation" on *Castles*, Conran notes that "the great structures of Western music — fugue, rondo, sonata, variations — are not just arbitrary patterns but the living forms of imaginative growth". And there is nothing arbitrary about the structure of *Castles* itself; indeed the intricate structure of the poem, its variety of forms, and our consciousness of the poem as a structure become, it will be argued, part of its meaning. The thirty-six variations are divided into six sections, each dedicated to, and centred on, a friend or, in the case of the fifth section, the poet's father, each of whom had died in the dozen or so years preceding the poem's composition. Thus Tony Conran's Modernism comes together in the poem with his avowed role as praise poet, praise poet not to prince or noble lord but to personal friends, and with that role inevitably comes the role of elegist. For while it is very far from having a uniformity of tone or mood, *Castles* is a poem haunted by human vulnerability and death. But, again, the perspective is never simply personal and private. In "At Dolwyddelan" (Variation II), the friends whose deaths are commemorated in *Castles* pass before the eyes of the poet's imagination:

179

> My sight shrivels. I turn to run.
> Dreariness reaching back.
> Procession of all my friends
> Into that cry in the dawn ...

Dolwyddelan, a native Welsh castle overlooking the Lledr valley, was built by one of the rulers of Gwynedd. The poet imagines the news of Llywelyn's death at Cilmeri reaching this stronghold — "I hear them call, 'wedi marw'" — and the despair and grief "that cry in the dawn" caused, a grief that will echo down the generations. Thus private grief, the recollection of lost friends, is in this place interfused with a more profound sense of loss, and "my people" takes on deeper resonance:

> The procession of my people
> Calling up to me for seven centuries
> As the Cilmeri raven
> Wheels on the wing towards Dafydd in Dolbadarn.

As Jeremy Hooker has suggested, *Castles* is in some senses an elegy for Wales.[8]

The castles of Wales — Dolwyddelan and Dolbadarn, Beaumaris, Swansea, Kidwelly and Caernarfon — are the presiding presences of the poem, sites of power. They are the most explicit expression of the first part of the Theme announced in the poet's "Note" and it is here that the poem begins:

> 'Clear the trees first,' said the Earl. 'No point
> In giving 'em shelter.'
> The first nail driven in.
>
> The crying root wrenched free.
> Whey-faced dirt heaped to a hill.

The forest scooped out.

Naked shoulders bit with an axe.
Thighs pushed the shovelling blade.
The first stake

'I keep this motte,' said the Earl.
'The bare tump asserts me ...'

"Castles are instruments of social alienation, an alien power coming and breaking down the pattern of the people", Conran commented in an interview.[9] "A castle is a wedge in the soul" (VII) — in asserting his power, the earl does not just uproot trees but cuts off a community from its roots, disrupts its identity. ("We are the trees that he orders his men to clear. We are the crying root wrenched free", "Meditation".)

A wedge in the soul, but also "in the soil" and "in the coffers" (X), for inevitably political power means economic power: "Lands/ By compulsory purchase/ (Or otherwise) appropriated/ To service castles". The use of the contemporary term is deliberate, for *Castles* is not just about Welsh history; it is also about the operation of power, with the past acting repeatedly as palimpsest of the present. Thus in Variation XIV, set at Dolbadarn at the time of the Enclosure Acts, the land is "privatised" and, while the immediate context is Llywelyn's imprisonment of his brother Owain, when the poet writes in "Keep" (IV) "All poor claimants/ To be suppressed", in post-Thatcherite Britain the phrase surely has other political resonance. In his "Meditation", in fact, Conran makes explicit the link he sees between the operation of power in the feudal age, marked by the coming of the castle-builders, and in our own age:

The British state is explicitly the heir of that feudal

assertion, in the shape of its kings and its queens; nor is the connection merely heraldic. Class division and oppression in modern Britain inherits its law and its sense of permanence from the castle building kings and earls.

But the poem's Modernism, its multiple perspectives, means that it rarely resolves itself into simple oppositions. When Conran speaks of castles as "instruments of social alienation", he is clearly thinking primarily of Norman castle-building in Wales, but Dolwyddelan and Dolbadarn were Welsh castles. However, such building was, inevitably, still an "act of assertion", an act of power and control on the part of the house of Gwynedd, as well as an assertion of identity and independence. Again, while castles were sites of power and places of imprisonment, they were also places of protection. In "Keep" (IV), for example, echoes of medieval warfare at Dolbadarn are dramatically juxtaposed with modern warfare:

> Stone on stone, clang of iron
> Wrenching, blundering
> Men scream in broad daylight.
>
> The baby was born in the blitz.
> Leering incendiaries
> Scrawled on the walls. They had no shelter.

The episode is presumably based on an incident in the childhood of Paul Nicholson, to whose memory the section is dedicated; the last line of the next stanza, an anguished question the adult Paul once asked of his friends, echoes through this first section:

His mother lay on the kitchen floor
Cradling him underneath her body.
Will you die for me like that?

The protecting, keeping mother is associated with the protective
castle:

O castle my mother, womb
Of the aspiration in me ...

Out of the belly of war
Protect me, mother. Pussy-willows
Fleck the rock with gold.

The "act ... of assertion" of which castle building is one mani-
festation is, though, only "the first part of the Theme": "'I keep
this motte,' said the Earl./ 'The bare tump asserts me./ I keep this
land'". Then the poet adds bleakly: "But he didn't" (I). While
their past power, their harsh intrusion into the land is imagined,
the castles are seen in their present ruin, "Dormant or extinct
volcanoes of militarism" (XVII). While we see the Earl's tower
being constructed, we are reminded more than once in the poem
of the geometry of the castles' artifice: Dolbadarn is a
"Rhomboid, squat round tower/ On its rock" (XIII); Caernarfon
has "Polygonal towers, faces/ Of vertical shadow" (XXV). These
are human constructions, shaped not just in the face of military
and political force, but ultimately, like all human constructions,
confronting time and natural process. And shaped, of course —
the poem seems to insist on the point — of natural elements; the
poet registers the "Destructible wood and stone/ Of the castle-
builders (X). For these places are not — as one might momen-
tarily read — "Indestructible". These castles ultimately slide back
to their elemental origins ("... the din / of siegecraft, wood on

rock//Stone on rock ...") and the inevitable processes of time. "This is the second part of the Theme", the reassertion of the non-human. In the opening variation, the "tattering trees" are displaced but not finally defeated, for all the Earl's power; they re-root:

> In this winter for them, where will they hide?

> In the Earl's tump, of course. They tower,
> They tower and break. Their roots,
> Their roots step in the hill.

> And in the tower the cracks
> Are the rhythm of rooting.
> The walls lean out like a tree.

The ruins of Swansea Castle are "Dinosaur ribs/ Elbowing out from the rock" (XVI), detritus of those who once ruled the land. Dereliction and waste constantly counterpoint human assertion. In Gwynedd the slate industry has briefly — given the historic span of the poem — imposed its economic and political power but, like the castles, its last remnants are now "melding into the mountains" (XVII). But again the poem refuses to reduce its vision to one simple perspective. In "Castles like slang" (III), as the castle crumbles towards being "what it always was/ — Geology and the processes of soil", two children, one of them the poet's daughter, play energetically and joyously among the ruins:

> Alys, aged six, turns cartwheels in the court,
> Enfys, aged four, sings out from two-foot walls.

Joy counterpointing dereliction, innocence contrasting military power. But at the same time we notice the care with which their ages are recorded, for, we realise, these children are transient too.

"An earl builds a castle, a viking inscribes a rune on a stone, an artist paints a picture..." The third section of *Castles,* in memory of the painter Victor Neep, considers the assertive will of the artist. The opening of the section is as bold in its assertion of power as the Earl's ordering of his castle: "I Godgest made these runes" (XIII). For the Norwegian rune-maker the rune has magical, transformative power; he is a spell-maker. Runes constitute "performative" uses of language, in J.L. Austin's terms;[10] they are part of an action, of an actual assertion, not just a description of an action ("Why this performative thingness/ Of a barrow-mound in Valdres?"). This section of the poem not only considers the artist as shaper and constructor, but the way in which artists can be implicated in the power structures and economic ideology of their age. Again here Conran is engaging issues which are central to his thinking about the artist, including the poet: the way in which art becomes a commodity, created by an individual producer as part of the capitalist cash nexus ("English poetry has been built on the model of the individual taking his commodities to market", *Artists,* 122).

Variations XIII, XIV and XV are set at Dolbadarn, on Llyn Peris, a location from which, as Conran indicates, so much Welsh history, successive constructions of Wales, are visible: the castle (from which Llywelyn's brother, Dafydd, briefly ruled), the remains of the vast slate quarry, and now the brooding presence of the huge hydro-electric scheme, part of Britain's privatised "National Grid". Here Conran places two later "rune-masters". In "Enclosure Act" (XIV), Richard Wilson transforms the scene:

> The wand of the Grand Style he waved at it,
> Put framing arbours, made the rounded lake Peris
> Speculum Dianae, mirror of the moon.

Wilson's "framing", his imposing of an alien Grand Style, represents the taste of his patrons, the great landowners who were enclosing in a more literal sense the landscape of Wales, "Privatised/ By the crachach, the posh gods". In "Diploma Piece" (XV), Turner, "the little Cockney", sees Dolbadarn with a "prospecting eye", the pun making explicit the "[m]arketable intimations" of his version of Dolbadarn: "He launches the bolt of commodity/ Deadly down the slatey stream"; when Turner was elected an R.A., we are told in a note, it was a picture of Dolbadarn which he gave as his diploma piece. For Conran, Turner "is the prophet of bourgeois freedom, ultimately what he paints are the values of the free market, the winds of change" ("Meditation"). Neither painter shows an awareness of the history of Dolbadarn, as a site of Welsh culture; the work of both men is perceived as exploitative, the assertion of ideology.

Victor Neep himself, however, represents a quite different

Tony Conran on Offa's Dyke.

186

notion of the artist. Although his pictures, with their subdued colours and moonlit landscapes, appear often to look out from "deep/ Arrow-slits" (XVII) and although as an artist he too is inevitably a constructor, a shaper, Neep is portrayed as the opposite of the invasive exploiter. He comes to north Wales, rather, as a "fugitive". (His origins were in working-class Nottingham.) Here in the dereliction left by history — ruined castles, waste-tips and "a working-class/ Crafty and demoralised and picturesque" — Neep not only shapes his art, but creates a community:

He centred us.
His cottage was the hub of North Wales.

Bethesda, Caernarfon, Rhosgadfan. Metropolitan
Of painters, poets, dramatists

In the two languages. They were extraordinary times.
And we who are thrown by the wheel's force

Into the darkness, like sparks from a forge
– All of us – confess that fire, that hub rotating ...

He creates a "Metropolitan", that which "forms (part of) a mother country as distinct from its colonies" (O.E.D.); out of the ruins of Wales is formed something which is itself a centre, has its own identity, not peripheral or provincial to something outside it. A "metropolitan" is also, in ecclesiastical terms, a leader, but Neep, we notice, is one who influences others from a cottage rather than coercing them from a castle.

This concern with that which provides a centre, a hub, a community, ultimately a home, is a recurring one in *Castles*. It is a concern for those aspects of being which are destroyed by the kind of individualistic assertion that castles, and capitalism, represent: "trees, communities, the flow of the world, loving" ("Note"). It is a concern, indeed, which would seem to be close to the heart of much of Tony Conran's writing and has perhaps deep autobiographical origins, evident in the poem. To trace these origins one has to consider the poem's engagement not just with the local assertion of power but with the expansiveness of Empire. Conran's historical awareness is too subtle to see Wales as merely the victim of English imperialism; he is acutely aware of Wales's active participation in what was, of course, the *British* empire: "I think Wales has always been an imperial nation...[T]he Tudors were a Welsh dynasty and certainly there was no feeling of alienation from it as far as I know until quite recently".[11] The fifth section of the poem, "Empire Road" sees "the dragon's tooth" of Empire as having been sown, long before Bosworth, at Caernarfon Castle, Edward's "polygonal towers" being an expression of ideology, imitating those at "Byzantium the Second Rome". It was a potent site for the expression of imperial aspiration, a place associated with Cystennin and Macsen Wledig and old Welsh dreams, peddled by Geoffrey of Monmouth, of Britain as equal of Rome, descendants of Troy. On such potent dreams was the actuality of Empire built: "The idea of Great Britain or British empire was a bastard of the union between conqueror and conquered, Anglo-Norman militarism and British — that is to say, Welsh — aspiration and memories of Rome" ("Meditation").

But Empire is no mere abstract idea for Tony Conran, as *Castles* makes clear. "Empire Road" has as its epigraph a line from *The Dream of Macsen Wledig*, alluding to the legend that it was Elen, wife of Macsen/Magnus Maximus, who was responsible for the building of the great roads of imperial Rome: "*Elen thought to have highways built from one fortress to another*". In "Litany" (XXVI) she is invoked as "Elen of the Hosts", protectress of imperial roads and seaways, from the ancient Ridgeway to the "shuttles of light" on "the laid swathes of the M6" at night: "It is as though the crying roots, wrenched out to make the castles of empire, should pray for mercy" ("Meditation"). This section of *Castles* is in fact dedicated to the memory of the poet's father, an engineer who built railways in imperial India, and explores therefore not only the poet's uneasy and complex relationship with his father but also his direct experience of the values of empire: "I was born in India, so I suffered in my own body and my mind the pressures of empire. I don't want to be melodramatic about that but it is a fact that my parents were away from me in my boyhood and when they came back of course I had to face up to this new pressure on me".[12] Again, in this poem of multiple perspectives, the mythic is infused with the political, the historical with the psychological.

As the poet indicates in *Castles* and elsewhere, the Conrans' involvement with the British Empire was a long, complex and ultimately profitable one; dispossessed of their lands in Ireland by the colonising English, the Catholic O'Conaráin family "Then changed to prods", "took to trade and Dublin/ And married well. Always we married well". They became both anglicised and enthusiastic participants in the imperial enterprise:

> Officers of the king
> Found fortune and Englishness in hot places –
> Clive's India, Ceylon, Jamaica.

It is a family without roots — that word again — Conran seeing his family as suffering from what gardeners call "replant disease": "We exhaust a locale/ For the rest, for those coming after ... / Replant-disease. No option. Marry well, and move" ("Conran Places"). The poet's branch of the family ended up in Denbigh, in the shadow of Denbigh Castle: "The Conran family, to make up for its wandering, has always had a strong tendency to maintain a base camp, usually kept by a younger sister, where casualties can be sent, and older uncles come back to die"(*Artists* 112). Though Conran's father received the English public school education of his class — "He was *kshatriya*, warrior caste" — he was too young to fight in the Great War and so he

> married
> Not well, but for love; and built engines
> For the Bengal and Nagpur Railway.

It was here that the poet was born:

> For two years an ordinary ailing baby ....
> — My slippery smile as yet undiagnosed
> Cerebral palsy from too rapid a birth.
> ("Father and Son", XXVIII)

The lines are almost casual, at the end of the variation. But the fact of his condition meant that his boyhood was spent back at "base camp" in north Wales, with his grandparents. The poem shows the poet's father returning from India after twenty years, the Indian Empire in its last stages; again "the assertion fails":

> The bearer
> Begged to go home with him, to the memsahib.
> The Raj visibly collapsing. In Calcutta
> He'd seen gutted muslims pushed down drains.

The father travels, with poetic appropriateness, on the "Durban Castle". This practical man, whose career had been based on physical precision, came home to a son who was not only physically uncoordinated but who lived in a world of books and ideas

190

and was, inevitably, resistant to "this new pressure on me"; the relationship between father and son, the years of mutual misunderstanding, is movingly portrayed in the poem.

"I was separated from both my parents from 1939 to 1945, and from my father from my sixth to my fourteenth year. This had its effects on my growing up, as can be imagined"(*Artists*, 113). What strikes one in reading Tony Conran's account of his childhood, is a sense of separateness, even isolation: the offspring of a rootless family ("Each generation [of Conrans] rejects the roots its elders have tried — perfunctorily — to put down", he writes in his "Meditation"), brought up thousands of miles away from his parents, his own physical infirmity presumably further isolating him from many schoolboy activities. He was also "moved from private school to private school (five in all) until I was fifteen"; entering the fourth form of Colwyn Bay Grammar School, he was moved through two further fourth forms into a fifth in a few weeks (*Artists*, 113). None of this, one would have thought, was conducive to the establishment of feelings of security. He evidently did make friends, but, he writes, "neither school nor neighbourhood ever gave me a sense of belonging to a community. I had my own life, which was that of the mind and the imagination" (*Artists*, 114). Thus some of the reasons why the impact of Gwyn Williams' translations of medieval Welsh poetry, which Conran read at university at Bangor in the early 1950s, was so immediate and so profound may be apparent:

> [T]hey were a revelation to me ... The bright, formal, exciting world of mediaeval Wales became my other home. Hywel ab Owain Gwynedd, Cynddelw, Dafydd ap Gwilym, Dafydd Nanmor and Tudur Aled became my brothers, flesh of my flesh, blood of my blood. (*Artists* 116)

191

By this point Conran was already beginning to write poetry and in this brilliant medieval world to which he responds in the registers of familial bonding and community, he found a culture in which the poet is not an isolate, marginal to the culture's main activities, but one in which, in a highly structured society, the poet had a place, articulating its values at the hearth of the tribe. It is a vision of the poet's role, of course, which not only fulfilled a crucial imaginative need for Tony Conran in his early creative years — exiled to Chelmsford as a clerk, he spent nights in the public library with a Welsh dictionary he had found there, translating Welsh poetry — but one which he has repeatedly articulated and indeed attempted to exemplify in the decades which have followed:

> To an extent undreamt of in England today the Welsh poet was not — and still is not — alienated from his fellow Welshmen. He writes as part of the community ... A great Welsh poem invariably moves as if it had the whole community behind it.[13]

The words which Conran uses of his discovery of Gwyn Williams' translations are, again, significant:

> Gwyn Williams imparted to me his basic *muthos* ... According to this myth the old Wales had more or less collapsed with the Act of Union in 1536 ... Like Eliot's myth of the 'dissociation of sensibility', it was a story of the Fall, of Paradise Lost. (*Artists*, 117)

The allusion to Eliot links Conran to other Modernist myth makers, like Eliot, Pound, David Jones and Bunting, who, as Wynn Thomas points out, "professed their undying love for 'established' traditions that, on closer inspection, proved conspic-

uously of their own making".[14] Whatever the actuality of the role
of the medieval Welsh *bardd* and the tradition which followed,
and few people know more about that tradition than Tony
Conran, it has at the same time become for him, as writer, an
idealised and enabling fiction. For Conran is not operating within the formal structures of a feudal society; he has to create his
praise poems, those poems with which he seeks to "strength-
en...bonds" (*Artists*, 123), in a society based on capitalism and
where most art is, in his terms, commodity art. In a Wales, which
manifests modern, fragmented identity in a particularly urgent
way — and in a regime which avows that "there is no such thing
as society" — Tony Conran has to construct his own community,
as he, with characteristic acuteness, realises:

> I've got to create my situation as I go along and if I am
> a traditional Welsh poet, I am by choice, by creating
> something where there was very little before ... What I
> wanted to do was to get a bit more elbow room for the
> personal, for personal relationships.[15]

Thus, the Welsh tradition is utilised, uniquely in the English language poetry of Wales, in a strikingly Modernist way, and for
reasons which have profoundly personal origins. (Outside the
poems themselves of course — though ultimately not finally separate from them — Tony Conran has long fulfilled the role which
Castles shows Victor Neep as having played as a creator of artistic community; few homes in Wales can have been so much a
"hub" for writers, painters, singers and musicians as the Conran
household.)

Images of "centring", of the place that centres and gives meaning, of home and community, provide a recurring *leitmotif* in
Castles, a theme which becomes increasingly audible as the poem
develops. For example, the images which are associated with

Victor Neep are picked up in "The Wedding Poem" (XXIV); the poet, invited to read at the funeral of Linda Noyau a sestina originally composed for her marriage, makes a collage by intercutting the sestina with another, describing the new circumstances and commenting on the original poem:

> Metaphors in the poem
> Make their circumference the occasions where it's read.
> Centre is mystery, hub of all they mean.

The original poem mysteriously shifts its meaning. Images of "saffron-heeled Hymen" transmute themselves "as water was made into wine" into Christ the bridegroom; whereas in the original poem she was "home in the vow and city of Hymen", now at "the Zion of her funeral", Linda, a convert to Roman Catholicism, is at home in Christ. Eirlys Roberts, to whose memory the final section of *Castles* is dedicated, is, like Neep (and the poet himself), a creator of community. Variation XXXV is a praise poem:

> A court in Upper Bangor —
> Eirlys the lady of it.
> And before her, the good ways,
> The kitchen always open ...
> Vortex of Pedwar Ec actors,
> Mystics and Breton au pairs,
> Worldly Dominican friars
> And the cockfight of poets ...

The long Variation XXXIV ("The Sisters") — to simplify a rich and complex poem — uses the myth of Brân, the need to bury Brân's head "under the White Tower in London", to give focus to the movement of so many thousands of Welsh men and

women away from Wales in the 1930s and afterwards to seek
work, self-advancement and excitement; Eirlys's sister, Non, is
one of them, her decision not condemned but sensitively imagined and understood by the poet:

> You cried for air,

> Air and the open world. You ran from a claustrophobia
> That cornered you like toothache ...

>   ...Wales held no vision then, except the head
> Grey with death.

In the face of this cultural scattering and disintegration, Eirlys
stays, roots herself in Wales:

>   There was enough
> To stay, to colonise the bare rock of dreams,

> To home in on Bangor, make the language sprout again.
> Teach. Act. Sometimes despair. But make home. Make
>   home.

The impulse towards home and community is the opposite of
the self-assertion expressed by castle-building. The opposition is
made explicit in "Giants" (VII), where the poet visits Tre'r Ceiri,
"town of giants", an ancient hill fort in the Llŷn peninsula;
"Compared with castles, hillforts seem open and free. You go
there and you are faced with an archeological daydream of Eden
... This is where we belong ... what it means to have roots and be
at home" ("Meditation"):

> ...while we live

> Each of these cauldrons of dry stone
> Is capped with a kraal. Smoke
> Twists its way through birch bark.
> Moans of oxen hang round us like mist.

The dangers of sentimental nostalgia for some lost tribal whole-ness are obvious and, typically, the poet is aware of them; the poem shifts into a somewhat surreal image of the rocks and bones of Tre'r Ceiri, like some echo of the dry bones made alive in Ezekiel, stirring to "gasp and tear themselves in parturition". The pun in "Are our hearts/ Littered here" also pushes the poem back from a single perspective: this might be a place of birth, but it is another human structure in ruin now. But the element of longing, for "The warm belonging root of us", is perhaps more apparent here than at any point in the poem. And, again, one notes that element of longing in "Father and Son" (XXVIII): as the poet's father voyages home from India — the "sailors doing something communal on the fo'c'sle" — he writes a postcard:

> *I wish you were on board with your mother also. It would*
> *make the voyage just right. Perhaps some day & may it be as*
> *calm as it is with me here.*
> > *Love from your Dad. April 16th, 1946.*

— phrasing which suggests that the engineer father did not wholly lack the imaginative sensibility of his poet son. The poet, reflecting on his father's words and the situation in which they were written, is reminded of Dante:

> > *Guido, i'vorrei che tu e Lapo ed io — ...*
> > *Guido, I wish that you and Lapo and I*
> > *Could be taken by enchantment today*
> > *And put on board a boat and sail away ...*

"Is it only the phrasing that reminds me/ Of the young Dante playing at love?" the poet asks; in fact it is not just the phrasing, clearly, but the emotions which underlie it, voiced by Dante in lines not quoted: "...the desire to stay/ Together'd grow with the oneness we lived by"[16]:

> For if I had been aboard and my mother also ...
> Our family never had been split ...
> And my mother's love covenanted rightfully
> Between us by the usage of a home.

The difficulties of dealing with such personal material are obvious, especially for a poet who has repeatedly indicated his antipathy to a poetry which directly expresses the "suffering individual with his *angst* and his desperate subjectivity"[17]. However, the Modernist techniques employed by Conran ensure that the poem never lapses into the mere confessional; personal emotion is displaced by literary allusion, as here, or distanced and controlled by the very formality of the verse form and register. In "Egypt" (XXXIX), for instance, the mocking picture he gives of his boyhood attitude to his father is cut across both by Biblical allusion and echoes of the litany to Elen:

> By all the rigmaroles of Egypt —
> Nine, seven, five, three and one,
> *Mary of the hosts* —
> I hated him with the spear of the wise
> *Have mercy,*
> *Elen of the roads*!
> And wasn't I the sulking boy?

Indeed, as variation follows variation — as variation on occasion interrupts variation — one is constantly made conscious of the poem as a structure, of Conran's artifice in patterning the multiple layers of experience, mythic, historical, literary, autobiographical. The poem shows a technical virtuosity in this Modernist structuring of which few contemporary British poets are capable: a free narrating form based on blank verse is juxtaposed with formal litany and cossante; each section ends with a sestina; in "The Wedding Poem", as we have noted, one sestina is cut across another and, indeed, comments on the complexity of the original poem's structuring:

> Catullus and John's Gospel melded in one poem —
> Arnaut's sestina under-read
> With *cynghanedd* plucked for their wedding
> From Dafydd Nanmor's *gwawdodyn* ...

There is a repeated use of collage: gnomic questions are intercut with passages of fiction from a short story ("Triptych at Cathair Dhuin Irguis, 3"); Victor Neep's reflections on his art in an interview are interleaved with a brooding, menacing sestina ("That it was a Merlin", XVIII). In the final section, verse passages about Brân are cut across with Conran's letter to his publisher about his struggle to complete *Castles* and the effects on him of his mother's death. At this point not only does the poem comment on its own structural patterning, but that structuring is set sharply against its opposite:

> *I can feel my imagination closing up. And there is so much*
> *to do, dismantling my mother's life.*

The poet himself, like the castle-builder and the artist/rune-maker, is a shaper, an asserter; *Castles*, like these other assertions, cannot avoid the print of Conran's own ideology. But through its very technique the poem avoids the castle-builder's imposition of a single view; it is uncoercive, open to variety and multiplicity, reflects its concern with communality. However, like the castle, the poem is constructed, pieced together, in the face of natural process, the inevitability of the dereliction which is the Theme's second part. The poem's very form is part of its thematic concerns: the self-consciousness of its structuring manifests an awareness of its vulnerability. Even language itself is unstable, its original shine and bite inescapably worn down: "And the clichés die down/ In vast rubbish heaps of language" ("Castles like slang", III). On two occasions the poet himself enters the poem, the image created being bleak, comic, courageous:

> My entrance
> Is not propitious. Shapeless,
> Lop-sided, bald, my trousers
> Sagging, like a dodo
> Trying to fly.   ("Stage Set", V)

Part Chaplin, part Prufrock, there is nothing of the bearing of the "warrior caste" here; his own structure is as vulnerable as that of his surroundings: "In the formal verticals of ruin/ I am standing". He shambles into the poem again at Swansea Castle ("Hiatus in Swansea", XVI), sinking

> like a wino
> To the convenience of grass ...
> Plastic bags awry
> Sprawling on the manky laund of it.

The variation counterpoints the structure of the human body and its systems, imaged in terms of the surrounding city — "Like skyscrapers the bones stand./ Brain work. The pull of the heart .../ It all seems so much in order" — to the small remains

199

of Swansea Castle: "It takes all the energy that went into/ Castles —dinosaurs — / Even to salvage this much being big ..." Enough of the castle remains to focus the poet's attention, but even "As the structure moves into its future" one is aware of how much more vulnerable are those "skyscrapers", images of the human body's fragile efficiency. The only human present is the poet, sprawled ungainly on the "manky laund". And always beyond the human figure is the otherness of the natural world, "the inhuman", indifferent, bound in its own harsh processes. It surrounds the poet as he stands in the "verticals of ruin" in "Stage Set":

> To one side
> Moorland in a scatter of snow
> Dips and climbs. Blizzard
> Has gnawed on the bone
> The high stonework.

This harsh landscape of rock and "rhyolite", "clints" and "bleached skeletons", becomes at times a fear-filled land such as that which counterpoints Victor Neep's words about his own art:

> That death came wintry amongst us.
> That half-mast flies this jack of a moon.
> That the day bit into us, right to the bone.
> That the fear, the fear, the fear, the fear ...
> That the merlin flew low on the hill.
> ("That it was a Merlin", XVIII)

The birds in the poem, often vividly described, are frequently an ominous presence: "Black choughs sound in the wind./ They are serious clowns./ They have messages" ("Choughs", VIII). In the concluding sestina of the second section, in memory of Mike

Donahue, writer, teacher and bird-watcher, his wife's image of him as a figure of integrity and vigilance reiterates the poem's nexus of castles/verticals/structures and is repeatedly juxtaposed to the fulmars who are "stylists" of loneliness":

> — Her image of how he was, a tall tower
> Private, stock still against the low hill and sky.

Competitive shades of the ripples hide them. Suddenly to the sky
Glide opens like a kestrel, flickering over the sea.

("Fulmars", XII)

In the fourth section, a potential alternative to the vision of human loneliness and homelessness is erected. Here the "castle" is that built "On the *maes* of Calfaria", at Dolbenglog, the castle built by Dai Pont, Pontius Pilate and at the same time a Welsh Everyman. This "carpenter's castle" (a medieval term for a wooden keep on a motte) is also Christ's castle, the cross, which bespeaks another form of power and the possibility of a spiritual home. It is a remarkable section, filled with impulses which are the opposite of the assertions of self and power elsewhere in the poem. Fascinatingly, given Tony Conran's virtuosity as a translator, the act of translation — "To translate a poem/ Is to walk in its land.//To translate a poem is to say, look" — is related to the "translation" of the Good Thief into Paradise: "Translation is a yearning thing, an act of faith, an attention to something outside yourself" ("Meditation"). The crucifixion as a source of comfort and consolation recurs in "Sandwiches" (XXI), while in "Linda" (XXII) the section's dedicatee, who had been given for adoption as a baby, finds herself able, as she nears death, to step aside from self and the world's values and to forgive her natural mother: "Forgiveness, too, is a hole in the continuum/ Of the world". In "The Way of It" (XXII), one of the emotional climaxes of the whole poem, the poet, urged by Linda's husband to pray for her, enters the Catholic Church in Bangor he has not visited for seventeen years, draws near to the tump of "Pont's castle": "And, seventeen years unprompt, in nothingness went in". The final part of the variation is a dramatic vision of Christ crucified:

> He was in a bad way by then, dehydrated
> With the sun and the staccato loss of blood
> As he climbed on the nails to breathe.
> 'I'm thirsty,' he croaked. So I poked an old rag on a stick
> And wet it in the manky, grey vinegar of my life,
> Pushed it towards him for his parched lips to suck.

As Christ cries out from the cross, the poet in his dream-like state feels himself "[f]lushed" with the "precarious joy that finishes a poem", filled with energy, "Before the dilution of time". "Old Mrs O'Brien", a "staff-room tea-lady at the college" and a fellow-worshipper, smiles at him as if welcoming him back and, in a wonderful piece of Modernist incongruity, she becomes Beatrice speaking to Dante in Canto XXX of the *Purgatorio*:

> Where have you been? Did you not know
> That on this mountain people are happy?

Here is another place to live in "oneness", it seems. But we need to notice that it is a "*precarious* joy" that finishes a poem, that time has the power to "dilute" such emotional climaxes. For this visionary moment, powerful and tantalising, ultimately appears to provide no abiding home; the poet offers no final credal statement, no conclusive spiritual structure to alleviate human aloneness. Towers reach "Into white air" (XXV), "a high-pitched emptiness" (XXVII), snowdrops grow "under a lean sky" and "in the blizzard of time" (XXXIV).

In the final variation, "Poem for Lesley" (XXVI), it is the poet himself who is the castle whose assertion stands in ruins: "my tower of fifty-seven years/— The broken ward and keep of it". But this final sestina, unlike the sestinas which conclude each of the other sections, is not an elegy. It is a poem of complex feelings, a valediction to his dead mother, evoked in a mysterious sun-filled vision of mother and child, and a turning to his wife; it is a poem tinged with plangent regret and awareness of failure, and yet, in the light of evening, expressing hope and love. But once more the single perspective is refused; the intimate, personal feelings are focussed and, again, displaced and controlled by the poet's use of the haunting, enigmatic thirteenth-century lyric to Christ's mother:

> *Nou goth sonne under wod —*
> *me reweth, Marie, thi faire rode.*
> *Nou goth sonne under tre —*
> *me reweth, Marie, thi sone and the.*

Reflecting, in his "Meditation", on the cubists, Tony Conran sees their rejection of the single point-of-view as having been "in the interests of truth: perspective and viewpoint were telling lies about the nature of our experience in the twentieth century ... Perspective trivialised our deepest feelings of duality. It made pain lose itself down the vistas of chiaroscura". *Castles* refuses to lie or to trivialise. It registers the pain of our modern fragmentariness, never ignores the vulnerability of our assertions of identity, nor the way even these can be implicated in ideologies of power founded upon division and alienation. But at the same time, in its uncoercive structure, in its imaginative inclusiveness, the poem speaks to the human need, in Wales and in the modern world beyond, to transcend our aloneness, to construct community, "to have roots and to be at home".

Notes

1. Meic Stephens, ed., *Artists in Wales*, 2 (Llandysul: Gomer, 1973), 122. Further references to this essay will be included in the text.

2. Nigel Jenkins, ed., *The Works: The Welsh Union of Writers' Annual* (Cardiff: Welsh Union of Writers, 1991), 16.

3. *The Works*, 15.

4. *The Works*, 14. Tony Conran, *Castles: Variations on an Original Theme* (Landysul: Gomer, 1993). All quotations are from this edition.

6. On the Modernism of Tony Conran's work before *Castles* and its relation to the gift poems, see Ian Gregson, "The Modernism of Anthony Conran", *The Welsh Connection*, ed. William Tydeman (Llandysul: Gomer, 1986) 186-208.

7. It is clear from conversation with Tony Conran that the elements in the second paragraph, "death ... what might have been", should be understood to be separated by "or". "Religion" is the basic impulse towards some kind of understanding of the world, not the construction of doctrine.

8. Jeremy Hooker, review of *Castles*, *New Welsh Review* 24 (Spring 1994): 66.

9. Ian Gregson, "Interview with Tony Conran", *New Welsh Review* 3 (Winter 1988), 19.

10. See Ian Gregson, "The Modernism of Anthony Conran", 201-2.

11. Ian Gregson, "Interview", 20.

12. Ian Gregson, "Interview", 19.

13. Introduction to *Common Ground: Poets in a Welsh Landscape*, ed. Susan Butler (Bridgend: Poetry Wales P., 1985), 13.

14. M. Wynn Thomas, "Revisiting Welsh Castles: The recent poetry of Tony Conran", *Swansea Review* 12 (1994), 21.

15. Ian Gregson, "Interview", 15, 16.

16. Anthony Conran, trans., *Eighteen Poems of Dante Aligieri* (Market Drayton: Tern P., 1975), [3].

17. *Common Ground*, 13.

Tony Conran, Folksong and Tradition
Ellie Jones

Tony Conran plays no instrument, sings not all, hardly reads music, and danced, when he was younger, only in private. Yet his profound love of all kinds of music – his encyclopedic knowledge of the traditional ballad and folksong, and his deep respect for dance, perhaps the oldest of all art-forms – enriches his poetry, his criticism, and all those singers, musicians and dancers who come into contact with him.

Hearing Schubert's *Unfinished Symphony* was a formative experience of his youth. There is no doubt that classical music has been important to his writing, which includes poems in imitation of, or as variations on, classical forms, like "Divertimento for Liz" in *Poems 1951-67*, for example, or the book-length works *Castles* (1993), subtitled "Variations on an Original Theme", and the recently published *All Hallows*, which has a symphonic structure and is intended, like *Castles*, to be considered as a whole.

Yet it is ethnic utterance, of all kinds, that has interested Tony perhaps as much as, if not more than, the polished sophistications of the great classical composers; and for a variety of reasons, not inconspicuous among them a need to search out patterns of performance in which he could feel his own writing and culture were rooted.

His fascination with ethnic music from all over the world, and particularly from Africa, India and the Far East, anticipated by many years the interest which has been generated in such music comparatively recently. He sought it out avidly, sometimes with

205

the willing assistance of his many friends all over the world, and sometimes coming across significant source material through happenstance.

The flame of his interest in ethnic cultures around the world has fired both his own writing and his criticism.

In the late 'sixties he found in a sale a book on a particular kind of oral African tribal poetry, *The Heroic Recitations of the Bahima of Ankole* (ed. Henry F. Morris, Oxford, 1964). As a result of reading the book, he wrote "Ebyevugo" (*Life Fund*, 1979), a gift poem for the wedding of some friends in 1972. In its structure it is unusual, even for its keenly experimental author, for it attempts to recreate the type of heroic tribal recitation which he had read about in his chance find.

Further consideration of Henry Morris's collection led him to attempt a comparison between the poetry of the Gogynfeirdd, the poets of the Welsh princes of the twelfth and thirteenth centuries, and the boast poetry of the Bahima tribe. In an article in *Planet* 99 in 1993 he compares those poems known as *gorhoffedd*, in which the poet boasts about his prowess in battle and in love, with the *ebyevugo* of the Bahima, in which the male tribesman boasts about himself. Tony suggests that far from being an aberration in the praise poetry of the Gogynfeirdd, the *gorhoffedd* may have been "a survival into the twelfth century of an earlier stage of praise-poetry". He offers the possibility that praise-poetry in the bardic tradition may have evolved from an earlier oral boast poetry, lost to us now, having been as ephemeral as the African oral boast poetry recorded by Henry Morris.

The diligence and care with which Tony has pursued this possibility is altogether typical of his intellectual rigour. His proferring of the idea is at once confident and tentative. "It may be objected that my use of the *ebyevugo* gives too particular a base to my argument," he admits. Yet his essay concludes in the hope that further research into early tribal poetry in other cultures may illuminate the understanding of the Gogynfeirdd and earlier Welsh poetry.

The same diligence and care can be seen in Tony's article on "The Ballad and Taliesin" (*Cambrian Medieval Celtic Studies* 28, 1994), in which he analyses some of the poems attributed to Taliesin, the sixth century poet, by applying to them a methodology for the study of ballads derived from David Buchan's *The Ballad and the Folk* (London, 1972). In this meticulous and challenging article, he makes connections between his chosen Taliesin poems, which are written versions of orally transmitted material, and other oral poems like the ballad.

Tony, who has been fascinated by the ballad form for many years, taught a course on the ballad from the early 'seventies until his retirement, as part of the degree course in the English Department at U.C.N.W., Bangor. There was talk at one time of setting up a school of folksong studies within the English Department, but the idea foundered through lack of funds and foresight; such a school would have benefitted enormously from Tony's guidance and expertise. It is surprising, and not a little disappointing, that despite all his knowledge of the subject, he has published hardly anything on folk music, and what there is has been produced since his retirement.

The influence of Tony's knowledge of the folksong and folk traditions of the British Isles on a generation of students was nonetheless profound. His years as a tutor on the ballad course coincided with the 'seventies Folk Revival. Although a roadside signpost on the way into Bangor proclaimed the city "The Athens of North Wales", it was in many ways a backwater. Yet in this aqueous cul-de-sac had foregathered a motley crew of people interested in folk music and song: academics and students, of course, but also musicians and singers from Ireland, some of whom had come over to work as navvies, rebuilding the Brittania Bridge.

The locus of folk activity for many years was the Ship Launch Inn, near the pier, which in the late 'fifties launched the City of Bangor Morrismen onto an unsuspecting world. The music played after the initially mostly Cotswold morris practices was not only traditional English but Irish, Scottish and some Welsh too, reflecting the mixed origins of the team members.

Tony's association with the Morrismen was long and close. Such was their respect for his knowledge of morris dancing that he was eventually elected to the office of Keeper, an office he still holds, although the team has long since disbanded. The office of Keeper involved the guarding of the Morris Log, a record of meetings and activities, along with other papers of significance to the fraternity, as well as attendance at the Morrismen's A.G.M., a notoriously and epically drunken event from whose more extreme and otherwise compulsory rituals Tony was fortunately protected by the respect in which he was held. His main role was as preserver of the records of the Morris community and as advisor on the actual dances themselves.

From the late 'sixties onwards Tony became increasingly involved in these local manifestations of the Folk Revival. His door was always open to anyone interested in using his vast collection of folk recordings and printed texts of songs and folklore. In his passionate desire to see the tradition of ballad singing kept alive, he guided many young singers to the classic folksong collection of F.J. Child, *The English and Scottish Traditional Ballads* and to Bertrand H. Bronson's *The Traditional Tunes of the Child Ballads*.

One particular group of singers and musicians met at Tony's house for many months, every Sunday evening, to while away the dry hours when the Ship was shut, in an attempt to put as many of the Child ballads to tunes from Bronson and other sources as they could – no mean feat, since Child runs into five hefty volumes and Bronson into four. They called themselves

Yggdrasil, after the Tree of Life of later Scandinavian mythology, and performed in local folk clubs the songs they'd learned at Tony's house. Yggdrasil dispersed eventually, as the members completed their degrees, research or job contracts, and moved away from the area. But they carried with them a knowledge of the British ballads to the four corners, thanks to Tony; in turn, they have surely passed on these beautiful old songs to others.

Another reason why this group met at Tony's house was that 'the session', the music in the Ship Launch, was predominantly and manically instrumental, except for the great surges of chorus songs. Some, like the members of Yggdrasil, who had played at the Ship, had felt the need for singing of a different kind, and thus had formed their group.

As more and more people began to be interested in singing unaccompanied traditional folksongs, and because the boisterousness of the University Folk Club became an increasingly inappropriate context for the more serious singers, it was mooted, partly at Tony's suggestion, that a singing club be formed, for singers only. This club, called Folk Circle, ran for two or three years in the early 'seventies, nurturing the talents of many whose interest in folksinging might otherwise have withered from lack of encouragement and opportunity. Tony not only suggested guests for the club, but put them up, and, with his habitual generosity, supported Folk Circle financially when attendances began to fall.

This club, although it lasted only a few years, was a brave attempt to provide a forum for singers, the like of which was extremely rare in Britain as a whole (the situation is not much improved now).

During the early 'seventies the thriving University Folk Club was largely an English-language event. With interest in Welsh folksong burgeoning, a platform for Welsh singers was needed, so a club was started by Dyfan Roberts and others, in which Tony was actively involved.

After any music session, English or Welsh, Tony's house became a regular port of call for singers and musicians. 1, Frondirion rang with music and song many a night, till the small hours, particularly after Tony met his wife, Lesley, who herself became involved in the Folk Revival as a singer of ballads and Welsh songs, and later as a morris dancer.

Bangor, the Athens of North Wales ... Bombast, true. But out of this little backwater many of the transient population, students and others, took with them the civilisation of Tony Conran's serious but impassioned interest in folkloric matters. The process continues in, for example, the encouragement Tony has given Bob Evans in his efforts to decode the Ap Huw manuscript in order to use the harps and other instruments he makes to perform early Welsh poetry as authentically as possible.

Why Tony's interest in folk studies? As a young man he had written plays as well as lyric poetry, but was discouraged by his drama-friends at college from pursuing play-making, on the grounds that he was "not a bit theatrically inclined". Yet surely ever since his student days he has been a poet in search of a theatre, a poet interested in poetry as an oral idiom, often in association with dance, visual images and music; he thinks of his poetry "as a dance for the tongue and the vocal chords", as he says in an essay in *Planet* 90. Hence the interest in folksong and its performance.

His interest in folk studies is important not only for his own writing. His intellectual curiosity about the origins of ethnic utterance has led him to build bridges between apparently diverse disciplines, and his willingness to share his knowledge of folk song and tradition has helped, in the words of his poem "Lament for the 'Ship Launch'" (*Life Fund*, 1979), to preserve the "long line" from danger.

The Collector

Alan McPherson

In the early 1960s Tony Conran moved into an elegant nine-teenth century terraced house on Glanrafon Hill. Compared to his previous flat he had plenty of space and a long garden. Within a few years he would fill it all. There were three ways to get to 1 Frondirion. You climbed Glanrafon Hill, you descended from the top or you came down the long alley from The Crescent and through the back garden. If you entered from the front there were two turns and steps up to the garden and the short path that led up to the door, then on along the corridor to the kitchen almost buried in the hillside at the back of the house. If you came down the back path you entered through the back-yard which had been roofed over, then into the kitchen. It was not an easy place to get in or out of sober. The centre of the house was the kitchen. Here there was always some form of on-going gathering. It was a long low kitchen not much used for cookery, it was dark, it was full of cigarette and pipe smoke, it was where all the gossip was passed on first.

When you moved beyond the kitchen you realised this was a house and garden of collections. Here were collected: (in no par-ticular order) books, ferns, records, Mozart K numbers, Schubert D numbers, tapes, Bob Dylan records, folk music, bal-lads, rhododendrons, hi-fi equipment, typewriters, and paintings by Vic Neep. There were a few works by Clive Walley, Mike Cullimore and others but the Neeps dominated. Here were also collected friends, students, poets, painters, musicians, the lonely, the depressed, layabouts, marxists, maoists, and a remarkably fine sub-collection of clowns, maniacs, con-artists, fanatics and lunatics. At the centre of all this was Tony in his dressing gown, often until late afternoon. If he was dressed then in summer he would be wearing one of his collection of short-sleeved shirts. In winter this would be augmented by a pullover from the woolly collection and that tweed sports jacket. Outside, if wet, a gannex and a trilby that had been too often dried on radiators. In the kitchen the kettle (one of a small collection) never got cold, Nescafé and sugar and milk and Players cigarettes were continuously in demand. Late-night expeditions would be dispatched armed with sixpences and two-bob-bits to gather cartons of milk and fags from the machines on the Holyhead Road. It was a place people came to to talk, or just be while the talk flowed on. Many painters including Vic Neep, Clive Walley and Mike Cullimore valued talking through what they were doing with Tony. Their time with Tony was important to them, it was a form of therapy, but ideas and obsessions flowed both ways.

Tony was a regular visitor to Vic Neep's house and studio in Rhosgadfan to see the work in progress, spend time with the family, buy work and enjoy the talk, drink and bonhomie as Vic and his friend George did their versions of Django Rhienhardt numbers. Vic Neep's work appealed to Tony partly, I think, because it was the work of a craftsman in paint. A friend of Vic's described it as "dog dirt and vinegar", but as Vic said with a twinkle " Very nice, I like that, humble discarded substances. I mean vinegar would have been wine" and the gravelly laugh followed on catching everybody else up with it. Vic's work was of pieces of discarded and decaying machinery set in an abstracted landscape, very like paintings of sculptures. Tony collected a lot of these and the later works concerned with Persephone of an abstracted recumbent female figure. There must be at least 20 works in his collection by Vic Neep; such sales would have been very welcome to a painter struggling to bring up a family in difficult financial circumstances.

If there is perhaps a deeper connection between the poetry and painting in general, it lies in the capturing of an image, in taking an experience, something seen, something felt, something understood, and collecting it into a poem. Many of the poems are visual capturings of moments, they could almost be short films of the imagination. Naturalistic and yet formal.

As well as the visual content, how the poems looked was also important to Tony. He published many of his own poems and was very particular as to how they would look on the page. The typography of the various books he published of his own work was worked out with care, every page had to look right.

The main collection of 1 Frondirion was of course the *Collected Poems of Anthony Conran* (now re-collected as Tony Conran). This was always being added to. Every week, sometimes every day there was a new poem or a revision of an earlier poem – though whenever he found the time and peace and quiet we layabouts could never imagine ... usually when the early hours shaded into the late hours. This collection above all others was obsessively sorted and re-sorted by the author into different groupings. You only have to look back through the various publications to see this sorting and re-sorting process at work. He also tried out many different verse-forms, and rhythms. Here are collected verse-forms!

This endless cataloguing was true of all the collections. People tended to re-arrange themselves into different couples, triples or other combinations but Tony was always deeply involved in the convolutions and re-arrangements. Whatever happened he had to be the first to know. Ferns in pots can also be re-arranged, why otherwise have them in pots? Another few yards of bookshelves enabled the library to be sorted out in a different way and the paintings went through periodic re-hangs as new ones were added to the collection.

213

Just down Glanrafon Hill and a short walk past the bowling greens into town was Bangor Art Gallery. This remarkable institution was run by the University in The Old Canonry. It was as remarkable and unexpected as the University employing A.E.M.D. Conran as a Research Assistant in the English Department. Only one student in the 1950s had gained a double First in English and Philosophy. He had then found the only employment he could get was as a reader of newspapers and journals for a firm in Essex where he spent his time looking for references to their products and working on his translations of Welsh poetry. Tony was rescued from this by John F. Danby (Professor of English) and L.E. Thomas (Senior Lecturer in Philosophy) who persuaded the university to create a post especially for him in the English Department. I doubt it would happen now. Just as I doubt a university would start an art gallery.

From its start in the early 1960s the gallery was an important part of cultural life in Bangor. Tony was a regular at openings and knew all the visual artists in the area. It presented the work of local painters such as Victor Neep, Brenda Chamberlain, Clive Walley and Mike Cullimore as well as the international avant-garde. John Latham's Skoob Tower of burning books of the mid 60s was both mad and shocking to a largely literary audience. Clive Walley's Tunnels of Lovely was an experimental art environment created in the old zoology buildings before they were demolished. It was, as Tony frequently quoted in the mid 'sixties, 'absolutely necessary to be modern'. He had finished his *Penguin Book of Welsh Verse,* and his own work became experimental with a series of poems later collected as Performance Poems and published in *Life Fund.* It was the time of the slogan, 'the medium is the message', which was true of much of the mainstream visual art of the time.

Clive as an experimental film-maker wanted to create a film around the poem "Aboriginal Song". The film sequences shot

214

near Beaumaris featured informal home-movie black-and-white footage shot by the Elliot family of themselves having a picnic on the beach. Simultaneously highly formal footage of the same scene was shot from the top of the cliff in 16mm colour. The two types of footage were then intercut. "Aboriginal Song" was performed at the Poem Concerts I produced for Tony in 1970 and 1971. The film lasted 10 minutes and the reader was instructed to declaim the poem at a randomly chosen point and to continue reading the poem over and over until the film ended. Both poem concerts involved a mix of live readers, live music, recorded voices and recorded music with projected images and artworks. The Poem Concert on the 22nd of February 1970 was entitled 'dial a poem'. We described it as as a 'mixed media event'. One section was a performance of the poem "Guernica". An audio recording of the text spoken by a narrator to music by Thomas Chatburn was used as a sound track to slide images from Vietnam along with pop art images. The second concert a year later, '0.125 Where is thy Sting?' (the time of decimalisation) included multimedia material from the first concert but was more theatrical in staging as it involved more live readers and a chorus, as well as musical soloists, and ended up as a jam session by Vic Neep and the Tŷ Gwyn Mob.

Mike Cullimore became obsessed with the story of Blodeuwedd from "Math fab Mathonwy" in *The Mabinogion*. It was this obsession that got him painting again after a fallow period. This was an obsession he talked through many times with Tony who himself became obsessed with it. The series of Blodeuwedd paintings (1974-5) led on to the great series of paintings created by Mike Cullimore celebrated in the exhibition "I am awake in the universe" of 1983. Tony wrote the introductory essay on Mike's work for the exhibition catalogue. This essay is a penetrating and valuable introduction to the complexities of the myths employed by Cullimore in his work. It deserves to be better known. Of the three Blodeuwedd paintings selected for the exhibition one was lent by Tony and another by Clive Walley. Tony's obsession with Blodeuwedd became the dance poem *Blodeuwedd*, first performed in Bangor, then Swansea, and later in 1983 in New Zealand. The performances featured the paintings.

As a collector of media as vehicles for his poetry Tony selected and used:

Music – Guernica
Radio – Day Movements
Poster– Space
Telephone – Dial a Poem
Film – Aboriginal Song
Slide-Tape – Guernica
Tape – Cybernetic Song
Chorus – Life Fund
Dance Troupe – Blodeuwedd

Tony's experimentation with these artforms led slowly to theatre, an artform where the text is only the starting point. Theatre draws together a variety of skills, some visual, to create an event in time with an audience. The gathering, the collecting together: to watch and listen to the bard.

And the latest collection ? Not one he made directly, and yet he is the inspiration for it. You hold it in your hand.

Conran's Brag

Jeremy Hooker

W. B. Yeats boasted of his friends. They were more than private individuals, of course; they were artists, such as Augusta Gregory and J.M. Synge, who were leading members of the Irish literary and cultural renaissance; artists who helped to found a nation. Yeats had much to boast about, and since he was, among other things, a praise poet, boasting was what he did well. The case of Tony Conran is similar, although with major differences, one of which is that Conran and his friends have defended a civilization, but have not succeeded in creating the Welsh nation of their dreams.

Tony Conran might be described as one of the last of the Modernists; a poet with affinities not only to Yeats (who recreated himself as a modern poet in his middle years) but also to T.S.Eliot, David Jones, and other writers who attempted in a time of disintegration to find or construct symbols of the whole. Not that we need to look for influences and stylistic similarities, (except to note that Conran, who is a master of the quatrain, evidently learned from Eliot's use of the form). The Modernism to which I am referring is not only a matter of linguistic and formal inventiveness, although it is also that, and in this respect Tony Conran is, next to David Jones, the outstanding experimentalist among Anglo-Welsh poets. It is also a matter of self-creation, of forging an identity as man and poet, of making a life; and the usual form this takes is that of finding or creating a tradition, an order larger than the self, to which the self belongs, and from which it receives its identity. There is no contradiction between this and love, and the feeling love gives not of choosing but of being chosen.

The idea might be summed up by saying that Tony Conran, who was born in India, born to empire, but from an early age chose Wales, fell in love with the Welsh tradition. Love has Romantic connotations, which are not out of place here. Indeed Romantic and Modernist are not polar opposites. Conran's earlier work reveals a poet whose affinities are with a modern Romantic such as Robert Graves of *The White Goddess*; and Conran has remained a love poet, in the sense that he finds his subject outside himself, in his relation to the beloved other, rather than in the realm of introspection. It is in his love of Wales that he has created his poetic identity. Wales that consists of individual persons who create it; the historical community; the civilization; the hallowed terrain.

Tony Conran is a master translator in more than one sense of the word. Most obviously, the man who (with Gwyn Williams and Joseph P. Clancy) has created Welsh poetry for the non-Welsh-speakers or -readers of our time. But there is also another meaning of the word that applies to Tony Conran. He has made himself as a poet by translating what he has learned from the Welsh language, poetry and culture into poetry written in English. He perceived in Wales a civilization "radically different from the English" (*Welsh Verse*, Preface to Second Edition); a civilization whose "defining art" is "the tradition of Taliesin", praise-poetry whose main subject is "the second person - you". In the Preface from which I am quoting, published in 1986, Conran says of praise-poetry, "I think I'd now want to call it "boast-poetry". It brags of its subject who is nearly always imagined as listening". Hence the title of my essay. In his later poetry, which has grown out of his earlier work (we are concerned here not with occasional poems or even occasional volumes but with developing lifework), in *Castles* and in his latest book, *All Hallows*, subtitled 'Symphony in Three Movements', Conran brags of his friends. As in the case of Yeats, however, he doesn't boast of his friends as private individuals alone, but of what they have done for Wales, politically, and, above all, imaginatively.

Conran finds in praise-poetry "a criterion of whole speaking, of making poetry as a private person, a social being and an objective observer – all at once". His concern is with wholeness in this sense, with the Welsh person as a whole being. But how is that possible if there is no complete Welsh nation? How, especially, is it possible for the 'Anglo-Welsh', for those who in their literary work claim "cousinship", that they are "a poor but honorable relation of Welsh", and among whom Tony Conran firmly places himself? (See his essay "'Anglo-Welsh" Revisited', *Planet*, 108.) A boast need not celebrate victors; from Aneirin to the present-day Welsh boasts are, more often, of heroic and honourable defeat. A boast need not be conceited or vain. It may raise questions about its subjects, or with them, in a dialogic form. It may not be about something that is over, like the raid on Catraeth, or the Battle of Mametz Wood (in *In Parenthesis*), but about a movement that is beginning, or a process underway. It may be about defeat followed by regrouping, as in Wales after "the days of the great dismay, the Referendum of St David's Day 1979" (*Welsh Verse*, Preface to Second Edition). Thus it is in *All Hallows*: defeat and death are remembered, but from them springs the hope of an imagined wholeness, of life and work given, laid down for that which eternally exists, yet constantly remains to be created.

Nor does a boaster or bragger need to be someone who feels completely at home in a culture. Tony Conran has described himself as a man uncertain of his "tribal credentials", and as "the nearest thing to an Anglo-Welshman I've ever met, tribally, linguistically, culturally". But he does not see this as a misfortune.

'Anglo-Welsh' designates "a frontier". "Like a tree that is living only in its rind, a frontier is no bad place for an artist to be." ("'Anglo-Welsh' Revisited".) Tony Conran's counterpart is Bobi Jones. The latter learned Welsh, and made himself into a Welsh poet, with all the vigour and freshness of the imagination reborn in another language. Conran accepted the Anglo-Welsh situation, and has been enormously inventive in exploring its possibilities and meeting its challenges. His commitment to Wales is second to none.

All Hallows is a "Symphony in Three Movements". The first Movement, "The Shadow", is about Raymond Garlick. Or rather it is, in the main, second-person poetry, in which Conran conducts a kind of dialogue with his fellow Anglo-Welsh poet. Garlick and Conran have a great deal in common so that in reflecting on his friend's life and struggles Conran is also reflecting on his own, and on their shared situation. Raymond Garlick originally came from outside Wales. He became, in the words of Conran's biographical note on him, "a Catholic and a Welsh nationalist committed to the formation of a bilingual Welsh state as part of Europe and the United Nations". Conran begins with a poem about Garlick's *Collected Poems*, "Forty years of you". Forty years of a "journey", a pilgrimage, into Wales. The poems in this Movement focus in particular upon a poet who is a pacifist, a man of peace, but who has a devotion to the Catholic Martyrs; a man whom political events, especially the rise of the Welsh Language Society, drew towards "the sort of patriotic heroism represented by the sixth century Aneirin and the warriors of the Gododdin".

In writing about (or to) Raymond Garlick, Tony Conran is addressing a poet whose poetry is lifework, wrought in response to the struggle for Welsh nationhood over a period of forty years. One of Conran's methods, evident throughout his later work, involves use of *The Mabinogion*. In a way that is characteristic of

Welsh and Irish poets (David Jones and Yeats again come to mind), he uses figures and incidents from Celtic story to mythologize history and his and his friends' involvement in it. It is a method that corresponds to the heroic ideal, and to the poet's function according to Aneirin: "Poets of the world/Judge the brave". As a voice of his civilization, the poet judges not only heroes but also the failures of his people, "The Waste in the chittering slates,/In the God, in the people/Eroding to Scree,//In the land, in the language"; their demoralization (the Referendum and its aftermath). But judgement is not the poet's only function.

Tony Conran uses myth inventively, and is himself, in somewhat Blakean fashion, a myth-maker. Thus, in "The Shadow", he adapts the dialogue between God and Satan in The Book of Job, a dialogue whose object is the testing of Job, to a dialogue between the Shadow and Imagination, in which the trials of Raymond Garlick as man and poet are the object. The Anglo-Welsh poet's position (Garlick's and Conran's) is as vulnerable as it is significant, and significant because vulnerable. In "'Anglo-Welsh' Revisited" Conran links himself with Garlick as "writers who were uncertain of their tribal credentials". In "Curriculum Vitae", a poem in "The Shadow", he describes Garlick as "A kind, principled outsider/In Wales, gradually/ Rooting in the green and white/Peace that you wanted". In another poem, reflecting on Garlick's years in Holland, Conran says that Garlick found there for a time "easier/Less compromising/Strangeness". It is in their situation on a "frontier", as strangers and outsiders to the land they love, that the Anglo-Welsh poets contribute most to the creation of the Welsh nation.

With the Referendum, it seemed that "the Shadow" had won; the Welsh people were demoralized, poets who had entertained great hopes, such as Raymond Garlick, were silenced. Instead of the celebratory festival, the raucous fairground. The festival, or feast, is Tony Conran's central symbol of union. It is a Christian symbol, which he uses early on in his work, and develops, with pagan associations, as a symbol of joyous communion, nationhood, in the context of sacred cosmic order. But Imagination's festival, at the end of "The Shadow", is an occasion of suffering and pain. It is associated with another great symbol of life, the Tree, which is "withered", "and the lips on its branches/Cry of dishonour, like a grey defilement/Over the land". This Tree, that might have been for the healing of nations, symbolizes a nation that is itself in need of healing. It is thus that the poet judges. The role that the first Movement finally emphasises, however, is that of the poet as healer. "Will he heal me like a poet?" asks Imagination. The Anglo-Welsh poet, represented by Raymond Garlick, is both judge and healer. Wales is truly the imagined nation, indeed *All Hallows* identifies Wales with Imagination. The poet is one whose capacities as judge and healer unite in the faculty of imagination, which shapes, makes whole.

Tony Conran has always been a risk-taking poet. The way in which he mythologises history is risky, as is his use of great symbols, and the way in which he connects both to his life and times. Happily his imagination runs to the grotesque, so that he is able to deal with painful experience, which might otherwise seem self-aggrandizing, humorously, as when in "Referendum" he refers to "Ianws the Yank" (Jon Dressel), "Raymond Cymro-Sais", "O'Conaráin" (himself), "Tripp in Caerdydd". These are indeed among his comrades; but without the wit the references would seem merely clannish. This risk-taking, though, is one reason why Conran is important: he has large ambitions, and doesn't lack poetic courage, which sometimes requires outrage. I have reservations about the use of Raymond Garlick's more personal experience in "The shadow", on the grounds that it seems more appropriate that Garlick should write about it, (as he has). On the other hand the treatment of Garlick (and Conran is a comrade who treats his subject as an equal) raises the Anglo-Welsh situation to one of the utmost seriousness; as Yeats and MacDiarmid treated the situation of their nations.

I have another reservation about the second Movement of *All Hallows*, "Soldier (a Christmas scherzo) and Investiture (trio)". This consists of a number of short poems, which, in analysing the soldier's role in the world, act as a bridge between the first Movement, with its emphasis on pacifism, and the third Movement, which treats a more militant activism. It is certainly part of the architecture of the whole book. I find it, however, more intellectually teasing than imaginatively compelling. Tony Conran is a poet with a powerful intellect. He has few equals among his contemporaries for constructive and analytic critical thinking. This is one reason why each of his books of poems is a whole and why he deploys myth successfully, with a command of both analogy and large-scale, intricately detailed structure. There is something in him of the system-maker, like Blake or Yeats. Indeed, Conran is an uncompromising thinker, a ruthless judge of what he regards as 'waste' or evil. He is, in this respect, a fundamentalist thinker, influenced by Marxism as well as Catholicism. He is a marvellous host to his friends in his poetry, passionately loyal to comrades, and unsparing of opponents. At times, in my view, imaginative system lapses towards intellectual scheme in his work, especially in the latter respect. I feel this is what happens in his treatment of the painters Wilson and Turner in *Castles*; and in the second Movement of *All Hallows*.

If I must register some disappointment with this part of the book, it is immediately forgotten when I turn to the third Movement, "All Hallows", and the poetic authority that is, immediately, compelling and moving:

> It is your new year's day, the first
> Of our winter, All Hallows,
> When the quick darkening autumn

223

Swings ajar, and the ghosts come.

Like a dark stranger I knock.
Paul, I bring in my ignorance
The new year. Now, your whiteness
Open. We must give gifts and bless -

To your further side of death
That glitters in the eclipse
So that one could almost swear
Light's bent from its corona,

And one sees for a second
The crowded windows, the good
Master and mistress within,
And welcome for our wassail ...

The poems in this part of the book comprise "a wassail", a ritual song which, Conran notes, means "be hale". It is "For Paul
Davies", not 'in memory of' Paul Davies, who died while still a
young man. For this is not elegy but praise, and therefore second-person poetry. As befits a wassail, it is about healing, making
whole, and the role of the imagination in this. Like the poems
addressed to Raymond Garlick, but with a more tragic intensity
it is about the cost of his healing to the healer, and the virulence
of the disease, and healing as an art that needs to be practised in
the present, if there is to be a future. It is both a new work in
which Conran breaks fresh ground, and a powerful summary of
his art of giving and blessing, his art of a civilisation which, like a
wassail, is of a form that integrates pagan and Christian elements.

Paul Davies was a founder of Beca, or (I quote Conran's biographical note on his friend) "Becca in English (after the nine-

teenth century Rebecca riots against toll-gates), to provide a platform for radical and nationalist artists". Paul Davies's own art-works included maps. "Maps of Wales," Conran says, "probably dominated everything he did". Paul Davies was "a committed Christian"; his "landscape maps" were not confined to Wales, and "the shape of the Holy Land claimed him as his religious apprehension deepened". Appropriately Conran finds his symbols in his subject. Breaking down gates and making maps are the dominant motifs in "All Hallows".

The gate is the gate of social injustice, in the time of Thatcherism, that Paul Davies and Beca attempt to break down; and the gate of nationalist demoralization, after the dismay of the Referendum. It is the gate between despair and hope, and between the past and the future. It is also the gate between life and death, the living and the dead. Like Vernon Watkins in "The Ballad of the Mari Lwyd", Tony Conran employs the symbol of the "holy Mary or Mare" used in the south Wales Christmas or New Year ritual. Partly in consequence of this and other 'primitive' elements, his poems in this part of the book have an uncanny quality, or the feeling of a 'frontier' situation, in which the living and the dead speak with each other, and exchange energies. "It is time for the shape of Wales/To have a future," Conran says. And, in another poem, "Wales is like perspective, it describes the space/imagination is using". It is this 'space' that Conran inhabits with his friends, living and dead; all the makers of imaginative maps, as he too is such a maker. This is the space of civilization, which survives only insofar as it is constantly remade, with gifts and blessings. Thus he can write, of Paul Davies:

> The Wales he made at Aber Alaw
> In a rockgarden of wildlings
> Climbs out of the night.

It is starry, it is Ephrath

It is where Ann listened at Dolwar
To wassail of Methodists
On their wild travels.

It is Llanddewi-Brefi, a raised
Earth, a pulpit
For a blackbird or a saint.

It is Zion, it is clear water.

"All Hallows", the poem and the book as a whole, is not, therefore a lament for the makers, for although Conran is capable of
elegy, his commemorations are in fact celebrations. What they
celebrate, what they brag about, are friends. And the friends represent a civilization, which doesn't consist of "broken statues"
and "a few thousand battered books", as Ezra Pound conceived
of the Europe of the First World War, but of an eternally creative
present, which works through Paul Davies and his landscape
map near the grave of Branwen, and through Ann Griffiths, and
through Dewi Sant. Anyone who has read Tony Conran with
care will know that he is a political poet, with a keen awareness of
historical and social issues and the ideological shifts of material
power. It should be at least equally evident that the Wales he
boasts of is a sacred country; in the words of "Was It So?", "the
bro of summer stars". His conception of this terrain has not
been easily won, and is not held without difficulty. In identifying
Wales with Imagination in *All Hallows*, Tony Conran is not so
much bragging of a great achievement, (although he is also
doing that), as celebrating the kinds of effort and sacrifice that
are required for the making of a nation.

Green Man
Gillian Clarke

Male Fern. Lady Fern. Moonwort.

In your library I could have sworn I heard
the rustle of ferns rooting in deep crevasses,
the hot crackle of spores, a gasp of melting snow.
High-ledged among the spines of Yeats, R.S, Sorley,
the Mabinogi's nourishing streams, wilderness
greened in the stagnant water of jars.

Hart's Tongue. Lemon-Scented. Maidenhair.

Later, that wet midsummer night – never mind
the rain – you made me climb your mountain garden,
a bit of pre-Cambrian half tamed by the suburb.
The two of us tottered up, up, in a stumble
through a drench of ferns and sweet mock orange,
and turned to see the glittering run of the Straits.

Polypody. Adder's Tongue. Brake.

I squint through a glass at the flipside of ferns – ovaries,
seed-sacs along each backbone like roe.
Like your poet's hands, that planted a public road
with rhododendron and scented azalea,
foxed as the pages of old books with spores
for the making of poems, gardens, daughters.

Tony Conran: A Bibliography
Tony Brown

Critical Books
The Cost of Strangeness: Essays on the English Poets of Wales. Llandysul: Gomer, 1982.

Edited, with Introduction and Notes. *The Angry Summer: A Poem of 1926*. By Idris Davies. Cardiff: University of Wales Press, 1993.

Books of Translation
The Penguin Book of Welsh Verse. Harmondsworth: Penguin, 1967. [With a critical survey of Welsh poetry up to 1600.]

Eighteen Poems of Dante Alighieri. Market Drayton: Tern P., 1975. Limited edition.

Dafydd ap Gwilym: Four Poems. Market Drayton: Tern P., [197?]. Limited edition. ["The Grey Friar and the Poet", "The Seagull", "The Wind", "The Ruin", with a short introduction.]

Welsh Verse. Bridgend: Seren, 1986. [An enlarged version of *The Penguin Book of Welsh Verse*, with the Introduction lengthened to include the period from 1600 to modern times, and an appendix on Welsh metres added.]. Second edition, 1993.

Eucalyptus: Detholiad o Gerddi/Selected Poems. By Menna Elfyn. Llandysul: Gomer, 1995. [Tony Conran contributed a Preface and numerous translations to this bilingual edition.]

Essays and Reviews
"Dylan Thomas". *Omnibus* [U.C.N.W., Bangor] 44.2 (Summer 1958): 43-48.

"The English Poet in Wales, 1. The Alien Corn". *Anglo-Welsh Review* 25 (1959): 28-35.

Tony Brown

"The English Poet in Wales, 2. Boys of Summer in their Ruin". *Anglo-Welsh Review* 26 (1960): 11-21.

"The Dialectic of Experience: A Study of Wordsworth's 'Resolution and Independence'". *PMLA* 75 (1960): 66-74.

Introduction to *Triad: Thirty Three Poems*. By Peter Griffiths, Meic Stephens and Harri Webb. Merthyr Tydfil: Triskel Press, 1963. 9-11.

Review of Medieval Welsh Lyrics, trans. Joseph P. Clancy. *Poetry Wales* 1.2 (1965): 25-26.

"The Welsh Poetic Tradition: I, The Heroic Age". *Mabon* 1.1 (Spring 1969): 47-57. [First of a sequence of articles originally broadcast on B.B.C. Third Programme and B.B.C. Welsh Home Service.]

"The Goslar Lyrics". *Wordsworth's Mind and Art*. Ed. A.W. Thomson. Edinburgh: Oliver and Boyd, 1969. 157-180.

"Anglo-Welsh Poetry Today, Part One". *Poetry Wales* 4.3 (1969): 11-16.

"Anglo-Welsh Poetry Today, Part Two". *Poetry Wales* 5.1 (1969): 9-12.

"The Welsh Poetic Tradition: II, The Age of the Princes". *Mabon* 1.3 (Summer 1970): 33-45.

"Riches of the Tribe". *Planet* 3 (Dec. 1970/Jan. 1971): 68-72. [Review of *The Earliest Welsh Poetry*, trans. Joseph P. Clancy.]

"The Welsh Poetic Tradition: III, The Classical Age, i". *Mabon* 1.4 (Spring 1971): 51-57.

Letter on occasion of *Poetry Wales*'s 21st birthday issue. *Poetry Wales* 7.3 (1971): 24-27.

"The Welsh Poetic Tradition: III, The Classical Age, ii". *Mabon* 1.5 (Spring 1972): 31-36.

"An Unmusical Nation?" *Planet* 23 (Oct./Nov. 1972): 76-80.

"R.S. Thomas and the Anglo-Welsh Crisis". *Poetry Wales* 7.4 (1972): 67-74.

"The Writing of Brenda Chamberlain". *Anglo-Welsh Review* 46 (1972): 19-23.

"Anthony Conran". *Artists in Wales*, 2. Ed. Meic Stephens. Llandysul: Gomer, 1973. 111-23. [Autobiographical essay.]

"The First Anglo-Welsh Anthology?" *Anglo-Welsh Review* 49 (1973): 198-200. [Letter on *Lyra Celtica*, ed. E.A. Sharp and J. Matthay (1896).]

230

"Idris Davies: An Attempt at Assessment". *Mabon* 1.6 (Spring/Summer 1973): 16-29.

"Idris Davies". *Mabon* 1.6 (Spring/Summer 1973): 46-48.[Review of *Collected Poems of Idris Davies*, ed. Islwyn Jenkins; *Idris Davies* (Writers of Wales series), by Islwyn Jenkins; *Poets of Wales: Idris Davies* (Decca recording).]

"Hiraeth and After". *Planet* 21 (Jan. 1974): 73-79. [Review of *Exiles All*, by Meic Stephens; *The Boy Inside*, by Sam Adams; *Starboard Green*, by Bryn Griffiths.]

"Two Daniels Come to Judgement". *Planet* 23 (Summer 1974): 61-69. [Review of *Noth*, by Daniel Huws, and *Funland and Other Poems*, by Dannie Abse.]

"Translating Welsh Metres". *Poetry Wales* 11.3 (1976): 88-106.

"The Status of Welsh Civilization". *Anglo-Welsh Review* 58 (1977): 87-94.

"Music and my life as a poet". *Welsh Music* 5.6 (Summer 1977): 35-53. [Includes an analysis of Wordsworth's "The Solitary Reaper" in terms of the sonata-form contemporary with him in music.]

Review of *Incense: Poems 1972-1975*, by Raymond Garlick. *Poetry Wales* 12.3 (1977): 88-97.

"Gwyn Williams as Translator". *Poetry Wales* 14.1 (1978): 116-24.

"The Irish Book of Welsh Verse in English?" *Planet* 45/46 (Nov. 1978): 111-16. [Review of *The Oxford Book of Welsh Verse in English*, ed. Gwyn Jones.]

"R.S. Thomas as a Mystical Poet". *Poetry Wales* 14.4 (1979): 11-25.

"Lynette Roberts: War Poet". *Anglo-Welsh Review* 65 (1979): 50-62.

"An Introduction to the Pictures". *"I am awake in the universe": Paintings and Watercolours 1968-82*. By Michael Cullimore. Illustrated Catalogue to an Aberystwyth Arts Centre Touring Exhibition (1983). 10-32.

"Lynette Roberts: The Lyric Pieces". *Poetry Wales* 19.2 (1983): 125-133.

Review-article on *Dafydd ap Gwilym: A Selection of Poems*, trans. Rachel Bromwich, and *Dafydd ap Gwilym: The Poems*, trans. R.M. Loomis. *Anglo-Welsh Review* 75 (1984): 81-88.

231

Review of *Twentieth Century Welsh Poems*, trans. Joseph P. Clancy. *Poetry Wales* 19.3 (1984): 148-54.

Review of *Out of Wales: Fifty Poems 1973-83*, by Jon Dressel. *Anglo-Welsh Review* 80 (1985): 87-92.

Introduction. *Common Ground: Poets in a Welsh Landscape*. Ed. Susan Butler. Bridgend: Poetry Wales Press, 1985. 11-16. [On the Welsh poetic tradition.]

Review of *A Small Field*, by Huw Jones. *Anglo-Welsh Review* 82 (1986): 99-104.

"Difficult Terrain". *Planet* 59 (Oct./Nov. 1986): 89-93. [Review of *A Ride through the Wood: Essays on Anglo-Welsh Literature*, by Roland Mathias.]

"Gerard Hopkins as an Anglo-Welsh Poet". *The Welsh Connection: Essays by Past and Present Members of the Department of English, University College of North Wales, Bangor*. Ed. William Tydeman. Llandysul: Gomer, 1986. 111-129.

"Ye Bryttish Poets: Some Observations on Anglo-Welsh Poetry". *Anglo-Welsh Review* 84 (1986): 8-18.

"The Uncommitted Persona". *Planet* 62 (April/May 1987): 93-95. [Review of *Selected Poems*, by Leslie Norris]

Review of *Bobi Jones: Selected Poems*, trans. Joseph P. Clancy. *Book News from Wales* Winter 1987: 7.

"Imagination's Roosting Place". *Planet* 67 (Feb./March 1988): 95-98. [Review of *Selected Poems*, by Tony Curtis.]

"An Abdication from Time: The Collected Poems of Raymond Garlick". *New Welsh Review* 1 (Summer 1988): 49-53.

Review of *Taliesin: Poems*, trans. Meirion Pennar. *New Welsh Review* 4 (Spring 1989): 76-8.

"Anglo-Welsh Manqué?" *Planet* 76 (Aug./Sept. 1989): 67-84.[Review-article on *The Selected Poems of Bobi Jones*, trans. Joseph P. Clancy.]

"Waldo Williams's 'Three English Poets and England'". *New Welsh Review*, 11 (Winter 1990-1): 4-9. [A study, with a translation, of "Tri Bardd o Sais a Lloegr".]

"Cerdd Dant and Choral Lyric". *Poetry Wales* 26.4 (1991): 40-45.

"The Muse". *Poetry Wales* 27.1 (1991): 50-56.

"Modernism in Anglo-Welsh Poetry". *The Works: The Welsh Union of Writers' Annual.* Ed. Nigel Jenkins. Cardiff: Welsh Union of Writers, 1991. 13-24. Reprinted in *Bête Noire* [Hull] 12/13 (1991-2): 384-91.

"The Debatable Land: Tony Conran on the tension in his work between lyric and tragedy" *Planet* 90 (Dec. 1991/Jan. 1992): 55-65.

"A Welsh Strategy for Literature". *New Welsh Review* 15 (Winter 1991-2): 52-58. [On strategies for Welsh Arts Council funding of literature.]

"Ferns". *Planet* 93 (June/July 1992): 70-77.

"The Lack of the Feminine". *New Welsh Review* 17 (Summer 1992): 28-31. [On the lack of a feminine voice in Welsh literature after the ninth century.]

"What a passionate poet this man is!" *New Welsh Review* 20 (Spring 1993): 15-19. [Review-article on *Collected Poems 1945-1990*, by R.S. Thomas.]

"Tribal Poetry and the Gogynfeirdd". *Planet* 99 (June/July 1993): 47-58.

"The Lyric as an Electrical Field". *Poetry Wales* 28.4 (1993): 43-46.

"The Redhead on the Castle Wall: Dafydd ap Gwilym's 'Yr Wylan' ('The Seagull')". *Transactions of the Honourable Society of Cymmrodorion* 1993: 19-44.

Review of *The King of Britain's Daughter*, by Gillian Clarke. *New Welsh Review* 23 (Winter 1993-4): 67-68.

"Three Letters and a Postscript". *Poetry Wales* 29.4 (1994): 19-22. [Three letters about the problems involved in translating three short poems from the Welsh of Myrddin ap Dafydd.]

Review of *Iolo Goch: Poems*, ed. and trans. by Dafydd Johnston. *New Welsh Review* 24 (Spring 1994): 71-73.

"Fairy Tales". *Planet* 105 (June/July 1994): 87-92.

"The Ballad and Taliesin". *Cambrian Mediaeval Celtic Studies* 28 (Winter 1994): 1-24.

"Anglo-Welsh Revisited". *Planet* 108 (Dec. 1994/Jan. 1995): 28-34.

"Ieuan ab Hywel Swrdwal's 'The Hymn to the Virgin'". *Welsh Writing in English: A Yearbook of Critical Essays* 1 (1995): 5-22.

"Pilgrims From A Desert Land: A Study of Idris Davies's Two Sequences and Gwenallt's 'Y Meirwon' as Responses to the Great

Depression". *Fire Green as Grass: The Creative Impulse in Twentieth-Century Anglo-Welsh Poetry and Short Story.* Ed. Belinda Humfrey. Llandysul: Gomer, 1995. 37-64.

"The Poem as Symphony". *Poetry Wales* 31.1 (1995): 52-58.

Volumes of Poetry

Formal Poems. Llandybie: Christopher Davies, 1960. [Awarded Arts Council Prize.]

Metamorphoses. Pembroke Dock: Dock Leaves P., 1961. Reprinted in limited edition by Tern Press, Market Drayton, 1979. [The latter edition includes a new Introduction and a commentary to the poems, as well as additional poems, including "The Mountain".]

Stelae. Oxford: Allison/Harlequin Poets, 1965.

Poems 1951-67, 4 vols. Bangor: Deiniol P./Denbigh: Gee and Son, 1965-7. 2nd edition, in one volume with Introduction, 1974.

Claim Claim Claim. Guildford: Circle P., 1969.

Spirit Level. Llandybie: Christopher Davies, 1974.

Life Fund. Llandysul: Gomer, 1979.

Blodeuwedd and Other Poems. Bridgend: Seren, 1989. [Awarded Welsh Arts Council Prize, 1989.]

Castles. Llandysul: Gomer 1993 [Runner-up in the BBC Wales 'Writer of the Year Award 1993']

All Hallows, Llandysul: Gomer 1995.

Magazine Publications

Poems published in many magazines in Britain, Ireland and America, including *Critical Quarterly, Bête Noire, Stand, Poetry Review, Poetry Wales, Anglo-Welsh Review, New Welsh Review, Honest Ulsterman, Fine Madness, North Dakota Quarterly, The Jacaranda Review* and *Planet.* They have appeared in several anthologies, such as *Welsh Voices* (Dent), *The Lilting House* (Dent/Davies), *Anglo-Welsh Poetry 1480-1980* (Seren), *Anthology of Contemporary Poetry,* ed. Wain (Macmillan) and *The Poetry Book Society Anthology 1987-88* (Hutchinson). Some have been broadcast on BBC radio, as have many translations.

Poetry pamphlets
published by the Deiniol Press (and some others), 1962-74
The Mountain
Sequence of the Blue Flower
Guernica
Icons
Asymptotes
A String o Blethers
For the Marriage of Linda and Gerard
Dialogue ('Fishpaste' postcard)
Space - poster poem to a design by Ian Tyson
Three Lily Seeds
Christmas Song
six poems about god
Silver Spoon
Dial-a-Poem
Silver
0.125 where is thy sting?
Last year we built together
Visions and Praying Mantids: The Angelological Notebooks 1-7
Three Celtic Poems
The Margaret Book
An Buinnean Bui (The Yellow Bittern)

Theatre Productions, etc.
Day Movements commissioned and broadcast by Radio Wales, 1967; produced for the stage by John Cargill Thomson in Bangor and Cricieth 1968.

Blodeuwedd, a poem for dancing, produced by Anna Holmes and Bronwyn Judge in Bangor and Swansea 1983, and subsequently in a different production 'Created Woman' 1984, touring New Zealand.

The Vow (translation of Saunders Lewis's *Amlyn ac Amig*) BBC Radio 3, 1988, commissioned and produced by Adrian Mourby with music by William Mathias.

Branwen, A Revolutionary Tragedy, directed by Gilly Adams for the Made in Wales Stage Co. at Theatr Clwyd, Mold and at castles in St

Davids and Chepstow, 1989. She also produced several readings of the play in Cardiff and Edinburgh.

Selected Reviews and Critical essays on Tony Conran s work

Roland Mathias. Review of *Formal Poems*. *Anglo-Welsh Review* 26 (1960): 73-75.

John Stewart Williams.Review of *Metamorphoses*. *Anglo-Welsh Review* 32 (1962): 76-77.

Gwyn Thomas. "The Poetry of Anthony Conran". *Poetry Wales* 3.1 (1967): 11-17.

Gerald Morgan. Review of *The Penguin Book of Welsh Verse*. *Poetry Wales* 12.3 (1967): 48-52.

Philip Pacey. Review of *The Margaret Book, Poems 1951-67* and *Spirit Level*. *Poetry Wales* 10.2 (1974): 49-54.

Peter Davies. "Notes and Queries". *Planet* 26/27 (Winter 1974-5): 154-156. [Review of *Spirit Level*]

Jeremy Hooker. "The Poetry of Anthony Conran". *Anglo-Welsh Review* 54 (1975): 172-182. [Reprinted in *The Presence of the Past*. Bridgend: Poetry Wales P., 1987.]

Joanna Lloyd. Review of *Life Fund*. *Poetry Wales* 15.4 (1980): 71-76.

David Annwn. Review of *Life Fund*. *Anglo-Welsh Review* 67 (1980): 143-146.

J.P. Ward. "Poetry of Food and Humour". *Times Higher Education Supplement* 24 Dec. 1982. [Review of *The Cost of Strangeness*.]

Greg Hill. Review of *The Cost of Strangeness*. *Anglo-Welsh Review* 73 (1983): 82-85.

Ian Gregson."Anthony Conran and the inadequacy of the image". *Poetry Wales* 18.3 (1983): 70-75.

Phil Maillard. *Blodeuwedd* [Review of the performance at Swansea]. *Poetry Wales* 19.3 (1984): 106-112.

Ian Gregson. "The Modernism of Anthony Conran". *The Welsh Connection*. Ed. William Tydeman. Llandysul: Gomer, 1986. 186-208.

Stewart Brown. Review of *Blodeuwedd*. *New Welsh Review* 2 (Autumn 1988): 74-75.

Peter Smith. "Against Ovations: The Nationalism of Anthony Conran". *Poetry Wales* 23.2-3 (1988): 44-6. [See Tony Conran's detailed response to this essay in *Poetry Wales* 24.1 (1988): 61-3.]

Helen Lewis Butler. Review of *Blodeuwedd*. Poetry Wales 24.2 (1988): 69-71.

Ian Gregson. "Tony Conran's Branwen". *New Welsh Review* 6 (Autumn 1989). 84-85.

Nigel Jenkins. "In the Iron of Our Chains". *Radical Wales* 24 (Winter 1989): 22-3. [Profile, which discusses *Branwen*. The following article in this issue, "Myths for Today" by Penny Simpson, pp. 24-5, also refers to the play.]

Dafydd Johnston. "Idris Davies and the orchestras of history". *New Welsh Review* 21 (Summer, 1993): 16-18. [Review article on *The Angry Summer: A Poem of 1926*, ed. Tony Conran.]

A.M. Allchin. "Illuminations". *Planet* 102 (Dec.1993/Jan. 1994): 93-95.[Review of *Castles*.]

Glenda Beagan. Review of *Castles*. *Poetry Wales* 29.3 (1994): 58-59.

Jeremy Hooker. Review of *Castles*. *New Welsh Review* 24 (Spring 1994): 66-68.

M. Wynn Thomas. "Revisiting Welsh Castles: The recent poetry of Tony Conran". *Swansea Review* 12 (1994): 21-26.

Interviews

Ian Gregson. "Interview with Tony Conran". *New Welsh Review* (Winter 1988): 15-20.

Greg Hill. "Tony Conran Interview". *Materion Dwyieithog/Bilingual Matters* 3 (1991): 11-17.

Dafydd Johnston."An Interview with Tony Conran".*Modern Poetry in Translation* New Series No. 7 (Spring 1995): 184-97.

[*Compiled by Tony Brown, based on a bibliography by Tony Conran.*]

Contributors

Gilly Adams, who has lived in south Wales for most of her life, was director of the Welsh Arts Council's drama department before she became a founder member and artistic director of the Made in Wales Stage Company 1982-95.

Tony Brown, who lectures in English at the University of Wales, Bangor, co-edited (with Bedwyr Lewis Jones) *Pe Medrwn Yr Iaith, ac Ysgrifau Eraill* (1988), a selection of R.S. Thomas's Welsh prose, and is editor of *Welsh Writing in English: a Yearbook of Critical Essays*. He first sat at the feet of Tony Conran shortly after arriving in Bangor over twenty years ago.

Gillian Clarke, poet and roving teacher of creative writing, has published five collections of poems, the latest of which is *The King of Britain's Daughter* (1993). She was editor of *The Anglo-Welsh Review* from 1976 to 1984.

Menna Elfyn has published five volumes of poetry in Welsh, the latest of which is *Aderyn Bach Mewn Llaw: Detholiad o gerddi: 1976-1990* (1990). Tony Conran, who translated many of the poems in her bilingual volume, *Eucalyptus* (1995), describes her as "the first Welsh poet in fifteen hundred years to make a serious attempt to have her work known outside Wales ..."

Peter Finch, who runs Oriel bookshop in Cardiff, was editor of that challenging magazine of the 60s and 70s, *Second Aeon*. His poetry is collected in *Poems for Ghosts* and *500 Cobbings*. He is the author of the best-selling guide book *The Poetry Business*, and is a regular poetry performer.

Raymond Garlick, founding editor of *The Anglo-Welsh Review*, has published nine books of poetry since 1950. Gomer published his *Collected Poems* in 1987 and *Travel Notes* in 1992. In 1995/6 a monograph on his work is to be published in the University of Wales Press's 'Writers of Wales' series

Ian Gregson, a lecturer at the University of Wales, Bangor since 1977, has published poems, reviews and essays in numerous magazines. Next year Macmillan will publish his critical study *Contemporary Poetry and Postmodernism: Dialogue and Estrangement.*

Steve Griffiths lived in Ynys Môn (Anglesey) until he was 18. He works now in London as a freelance researcher in poverty and social policy. The most recent of his four books of poetry is a *Selected Poems* (Seren Books, 1993).

Peter Gruffydd, born in Liverpool and raised in north Wales, made his debut as a poet (with Meic Stephens and Harri Webb) in the volume *Triad* (1963), which carried an introduction by Tony Conran. Chatto & Windus published his full-length collection, *The Shivering Seed* in 1972.

Jeremy Hooker is Professor of English at Bath College of Higher Education, where he directs the M.A. in Creative Writing. His most recent book of poems is *Their Silence a Language* (1994), a collaboration with the sculptor Lee Grandjean. One of his four books of criticism, *The Presence of the Past* (1987), contains an earlier essay on Tony Conran.

Nigel Jenkins's books include *Acts of Union: Selected Poems 1975-89* (1990), an essay on John Tripp in the University of Wales Press's 'Writers of Wales' series, and *Gwalia in Khasia* (1995) about Welsh missionaries in north-east India.

Ellie Jones, Head of English at Ysgol Dyffryn Ogwen, Bethesda, writes poetry, sings unaccompanied folksongs, and has recently produced a study aid on the early work of R.S. Thomas for use in secondary schools.

R. Gerallt Jones retired this year as Warden of Gregynog, the University of Wales's annexe near Newtown, Powys. He is the author of five novels, plays and documentary scripts, four volumes of literary criticism and five books of poetry. He edited and translated *Poetry of Wales 1930-70* (1974), and takes a keen interest in Third World literature.

Sally Roberts Jones, current Chairman of the English-language section of the Welsh Academy, has published four collections of poetry, short stories, critical studies, folk tales for children, local history and bibliographies of Anglo-Welsh literature. She runs the Port Talbot imprint Alun Books.

Alan McPherson, (a.k.a Phredd) painter, graphic designer, photographer, film maker and cultural odd jobber. Lived in and around Bangor for 14 years until 1977 when he moved to Leicestershire.

Les Murray, poet and essayist, is one of Australia's leading literary figures. His most recent collection of poems is *Translations from the Natural World* published in Britain by Carcanet (1993). In 1992 Minerva published his *Collected Poems*. He is a frequent visitor to Wales where he has many friends.

Anna-Marie Taylor was a lecturer in drama at the University of Wales, Aberystwyth from 1982 to 1994, and is at present working in the Department of Adult and Continuing Education at the University of Wales, Swansea. She has published widely on modern European theatre and literature.

Dafydd Elis Thomas lectured in drama and literature at Coleg Harlech until he won the Parliamentary seat of Meirionnydd for Plaid Cymru in 1974. From 1983 until the early 90s he was the Party's President, and is currently Chairman of the Welsh Language Board.

Ned Thomas, director of the University of Wales Press, is a critic and essayist best known, perhaps, as the founding editor of *Planet* and author of the influential argument for left-wing Welsh Nationalism, *The Welsh Extremist* (1971). He has written critical studies of George Orwell, Derek Walcott and Waldo Williams.

M. Wynn Thomas is Professor of English at the University of Wales, Swansea. Among his numerous books are *Internal Difference: literature in twentieth-century Wales* (1992) and *The Lunar Light of Whitman's Poetry*. His most recent publications are *The Page's Drift: R.S. Thomas at eighty* and *Dail Glaswellt,* a Welsh translation of Walt Whitman's poetry.

Selwyn Williams, descended from a long line of carpenters, is a native of Dyffryn Conwy who has lived for the last twenty odd years in Llanrug in Arfon. He is a lecturer at Coleg Normal, Bangor. His chief interest is Welsh revolution: he is an active supporter of Cymdeithas yr Iaith, Cymru-Cuba, the trade union movement and Green campaigns.